Why Quantum Physicists Do Not Fail

By Greg Kuhn

D1114361

Table of Contents

Introduction

Many people don't read introductions. Obviously, you're not like most people. In fact, the act of reading this book, in my experience, makes you part of the ten-percent club. This is an exclusive club that, while open to anyone, is usually only comprised of ten percent of the population. Ten-percenters are the unfortunately small group who are not satisfied with the status quo. They simply do not accept that life is frustrating and their dreams and goals are destined to remain unfulfilled. As a part of this exclusive group, you no doubt have searched for answers regarding how to fulfill your greatest vision of yourself for most of your adult life. I have too. And I've never found answers as amazingly effective as the ones you're about to learn.

This book has some science and history in it. Don't fret if you're not excited about those topics. I include them to give you a frame of reference for why the information you're about to learn is so different, so important, and so relevant. When you're finished with this book, I believe you'll understand that what you've learned is not simply one person's philosophy but, actually, a logical next-step for anyone's personal evolution—an evolution that will eventually be happening for the entire Western world.

This is a self-help book about using quantum physics to achieve your dreams and goals. But it's more precise to refer to it as a book about using new paradigms from quantum physics. I'm confident in the accuracy of the science you'll read and learn in this book; I hope it fascinates you as much as it does me. But I also willingly confess I'm not a physicist—nor even a scientist. I am a science "nerd" and a history teacher who has held a lifelong fascination with learning about the reasons people do things the way they do them. I am also a futurist, which, in my case, means I am an author who writes about new paradigms from quantum physics that have yet to be adopted by the mainstream. Rest assured that these new paradigms are based on an amazingly precise body of science (quantum physics, of course) that has created a second scientific revolution. And these new paradigms will soon become the conventional wisdom of your children and grandchildren.

Because you're reading this book now, however, you won't have to wait until these paradigms are universally adopted; you get to be an early adopter and start experiencing, right now, amazing success at achieving your goals and dreams more completely than you've hoped.

If what you learn about quantum physics here excites you as much as it does me, you should explore quantum physics in greater depth by reading some of the authors I follow with devotion. For starters, I highly recommend: Brian Greene (*The Hidden Reality: Parallel Universes and the Deep Laws of the Cosmos*, New York: Vintage, 2011), Stephen

Hawking (*The Grand Design*, New York: Bantam, 2012), Amit Goswami (*The Self Aware Universe*, New York: Tarcher, 1995), Nick Herbert (*Quantum Reality: Beyond the New Physics*, New York: Anchor, 1987), John Gribbin (*In Search of Schrodinger's Cat: Quantum Physics and Reality*, New York: Bantam Books, 1984), Richard Feynman (*Six Easy Pieces*, New York: Basic Books, 1998), and Michio Kaku (*Physics of the Impossible: A Scientific Exploration into the World of Phasers, Force Fields, Teleportation, and Time Travel*, New York: Anchor, 2009).

This book is a great place to start if you're just learning about quantum physics. And, if you're already familiar with and fascinated by quantum physics, this book will give you some exciting new ways to think about and use this amazing science. Even if you aren't currently interested in quantum physics but want to learn to be a more successful person and achieve some heretofore unattainable goals, you will find some unique solutions here. Wherever you stand regarding quantum physics, the paradigms you learn in this book will fill you with amazing personal power and resourcefulness, turning your world (and the reasons you do things the way you do them) upside down in some incredibly positive ways.

This book is also a wonderful resource for law-of-attraction enthusiasts, and my books are quite popular with folks who study it. Although I have been interested in the law of attraction since the early 1990s, I have not titled my books as such, because quantum theory does not consciously attempt to either prove or validate this philosophy. I'm not certain whether quantum physics is describing the law of attraction or vice versa, but my opinion is that quantum physics does describe the law of attraction as it is being studied by millions around the world. Some people even call me "The Law of Attraction Science Guy," so this book should be a wonderful addition to any law-of-attraction resource library.

Chapter One: How a Failed Experiment Changed the Western World

"By far the most important consequence of the conceptual revolution brought about in physics by the relativity and quantum theory lies not in such details as that meter sticks shorten when they move or that simultaneous position and momentum have no meaning, but in the insight that we had not been using our minds properly and that it is important to find out how to do so."

Percy W. Bridgman
Physicist
Nobel Prize Winner

In 1887, two scientists named Albert Michelson and Edward Morley conducted a year-long experiment to measure the speed of the Earth as it traveled around the Sun. Michelson and Morley invented an interferometer instrument, able to detect light waves' interference effects, and spent one calendar year taking measurements of the Sun's rays. When they concluded, their results were astounding, and their experiment, by itself, literally changed the entire world.

Before we discuss Michelson and Morley's results and how they changed the world, it is important to note a few things about their experiment. First, like all scientists in the 19th century, Michelson and Morley used what is now referred to as classical physics to conduct their experiment. Classical physics is the science from the first scientific revolution, the science of Sir Isaac Newton.

It is the science you learned about in your high school science classes. Four of classical physics' primary principles are:

1. Each "thing" is made of smaller parts with predictable functions. The smaller parts play roles in making the larger thing work. That is their "job."

2. For every action, there is an equal and opposite reaction. Every movement has a cause. Every action is determined by something else exerting itself upon the thing that acted.

3. The observer and the observed are two separate things. A scientist, a teacher, a manager, an administrator, etc., are all distinct and separate observers of what they are observing or experimenting with.

4. Things occur in a logical, linear fashion. When a certain outcome occurs, you can always find the cause by tracing the multiplied effects backwards. Action is like a row of dominoes falling after the first one gets pushed.

At the time of Michelson and Morley's experiment, scientists believed that classical physics was so comprehensively correct that it had revealed, once and for all, everything there was to know about how our universe worked. In fact, scientists' faith in classical physics was so unreserved that Lord Kelvin (famous for his discovery of absolute zero) was telling his brightest students to go into a field other than physics because, he said, "All the important work has been done there."

And it wasn't just scientists who believed in the paradigms of classical physics. Great writers, statesmen, and thinkers used them to alter existing fields and disciplines or even create brand new ones. Adam Smith, Sigmund Freud, Thomas Jefferson, Frederick Taylor, Karl Marx, and Charles Darwin are but a few examples of the household names who applied the paradigms from the science of the first scientific revolution to other disciplines such as economics, medicine, business, engineering, government, or biology. And, through these applications, Western society, as a whole, adopted the paradigms of classical physics.

Now back to Michelson and Morley. When these two men tabulated their data, they discovered the speed at which the Earth traveled as it sped around the Sun. And what was the speed of the Earth according to classical physics? Zero miles per hour. Of course, Michelson and Morley knew this couldn't possibly be accurate and so did the rest of the world. For this reason, the results of this experiment literally rocked the foundations of the world scientific community. Classical physics, the science of the first scientific revolution, which had been thought to have finally revealed all the mysteries of the universe, had been shown to be inaccurate. Classical physics was, essentially, wrong.

Michelson and Morley's experiment is now referred to as the most famous failed experiment in history, because its results required scientists to pursue a science that could accurately calculate something such as the speed of the Earth. Classical physics had failed to deliver accurate data, and the scientific community was forced to go back to the drawing board and uncover a new way to divine how our universe worked. This quest opened the door to a new science and a second scientific revolution: quantum physics.

From the late 19th century until today, quantum physics has not only resolved most (but not yet all) of the mysteries of our universe, but it has also repeatedly shown itself to be the most accurate and reliable science ever created. In fact, noted physicist and author Brian Greene has said that it is probably impossible for humans to come any closer to knowing the inner workings of our universe than what we now know because of quantum physics.

Although we have had a second scientific revolution and the science of that second revolution has, generally, replaced classical physics as a source for answers to the quandaries of our universe, quantum physics has yet to be incorporated into our modern, daily lives in the way that classical physics was. There is not yet a voluminous canon of thinkers applying the new paradigms from quantum physics to modern fields and disciplines the way Smith, Freud, Jefferson, Taylor, Marx, and Darwin (and so many others) did after the first scientific revolution.

But those applications will happen because that is how new ideas from improved scientific knowledge are disseminated. Great thinkers will apply the science of quantum physics to every field and discipline in the Western world, and our paradigms—the reasons we do things the way we do them—will change. In fact, they already are. And, while I would never claim to be a genius like the men I just listed, this book is an example of how the paradigms from the second scientific revolution, quantum physics, will spread and will change every aspect of why we do things the way we do them in the 21st century.

The new paradigms from quantum physics that you learn in this book will allow you to address and solve some of your most vexing challenges and frustrations. By using these new paradigms, you'll have an incredible new wellspring of efficacy in your life, and you'll come much closer than ever before to achieving your goals and dreams. Even when following the same instructions for their realization that you have previously.

You can rest assured that these new paradigms, while perhaps unsettlingly strange at first read, will one day be the norm for almost everyone. Your friends and family may not immediately join you in adopting these new paradigms, because they have not yet become the predominant ones that govern the Western world. But because these new paradigms come from the most precise, accurate, and reliable body of science ever created, a science that has virtually supplanted the old science of classical physics, the entire Western world will soon adopt them, just as our ancestors adopted the paradigms that came from the first scientific revolution. You will simply be an early adopter of paradigms that will soon be everyone's conventional wisdom.

I congratulate you for your intellectual curiosity, your open mindedness, your willingness, and your desire to learn how to be a happier, healthier, more successful citizen of the 21st century.

Chapter Two: We Live in Fish Tanks

"In the beginning there were only probabilities. The universe could only come into existence if someone observed it. It does not matter that the observers turned up several billion years later. The universe exists because we are aware of it."

Martin Rees
Astrophysicist

In 1962, while a professor at the University of California, Berkeley, Thomas Kuhn wrote his most famous book, *The Structure of Scientific Revolutions*. In this book, Kuhn coined a new term that quickly entered into our lexicon: paradigm shift. Kuhn proposed that scientists need to remain open to new ideas that don't fit within their current constructs and framework. He used the term "paradigm shift" to describe a scientist's need to consider that her ideas about how our universe functions must continually be subject to revision based on new, more accurate scientific knowledge.

Part of Kuhn's thesis was that, since scientific revolutions usher in changes in scientific knowledge that shatter long-held beliefs, a scientist must always be prepared to adopt completely new frameworks to understand the universe. Or, as he put it, she must be prepared to undergo a paradigm shift so she can properly use the new knowledge in relevant ways in her work. Since 1962, the term "paradigm" has become widely used and is now universally applied by non-scientists as well.

We all hold paradigms through which we understand our world. And, as Kuhn made note, those paradigms come from the most current and accurate scientific knowledge available. Paradigms don't necessarily tell us **what** to do (they do not usually involve the nuts-and-bolts, how-to instructions for our daily lives); instead paradigms tell us **why** we do things the way we do them. Our paradigms are the umbrella under which all the things we do make sense to us; they are, in fact, the reasons we do things the way we do them.

One way I've found helpful to envision a paradigm is as a fish tank. And within this fish tank you are the fish. Of course, an actual fish would not only have no cause to reflect on why she is in her particular fish tank, but she would also have no ability to do so (unless this fish was a character from the Disney movie *Finding Nemo*).

But just as paradigms do for you, all the reasons why a fish does the things the way she does them is governed and dictated by the unique fish tank in which she lives. Why does she swim in the particular routine she always does? Why does she sleep where and when she does? Why does she eat where and when she does? The unique fish tank she inhabits is the reason.

Another thing you should know about paradigms is that they are not necessarily designed to last forever. In fact, since our paradigms are always formed by the best, most current scientific knowledge, our paradigms change as our scientific knowledge grows. This is exactly what happened to the world after the first scientific revolution. Those paradigm shifts allowed the creation of the modern Western world in which you now live. I'll describe that process in greater detail later.

For now, understand that the paradigms that people hold remain valid until better, more accurate ones arise from better, more accurate science. The world will always undergo paradigm shifts when scientific knowledge grows and improves. Paradigms have always shifted in this manner and always will.

So let's return to our fish tank metaphor. The fish tank in our metaphor is the home to a little fish named Splash, who has a burning desire to become a powerful deep-ocean swimmer. Given her dream, Splash investigates what she'll need to do to reform herself and her swimming abilities to achieve her goals. Splash finds a great book full of expert instruction, written by a champion tuna living in the Atlantic Ocean. The tuna's workout program provides Splash with step-by-step instructions which, when followed faithfully, promise to transform any fish into an open-ocean powerhouse.

After a restful night's sleep, Splash jumps out of her bed because she is so excited to begin the program. Already brimming with desire to achieve her dreams, Splash bubbles with anticipation because she not only has the willingness to work hard, but now she also has the expert instruction she needs to reach her goal.

But after following the tuna's program for a month, Splash has made only minor progress toward her goal. She has worked diligently every day, followed all the instructions to the letter, and her intense desire to achieve her goal has never wavered. Yet she has failed to reach her intended outcome. Splash is still the same little swimmer she was when she started. In despair, Splash gives up and, with a tear, sadly declares to herself, "I guess I'm just not cut out to be a deep-sea swimmer."

Splash tries to move on with her life, resigned to her fate. But, as is usually the case with our deep desires, Splash is never really able to say goodbye to her dreams. No matter how much she tells herself that deep-sea swimming is not her "destiny," that dream remains. So when Splash happens across another program a month later, written by a famous porpoise, she gets excited and rekindles her resolve to achieve her goal. "I must have had the wrong book last time," Splash enthusiastically tells herself after reading through the porpoise's program.

Splash does the same thing this time as she did last time. Powered by her renewed excitement and feverish desire, she once again works diligently each day, follows every one of the porpoise's instructions to the letter, and never doubts that she will reach her goal. Yet, once again, after a month-and-a-half this time, Splash is forced to accept that she has failed again. She now feels like a failure; she's not just sad, she now blames herself. And she doesn't just suffer tears this time. Splash spends two days holed up in the corner of her fish tank soothing her wounded psyche with chocolate ice cream.

Eventually, Splash recovers from her failure. And, over the course of the next three years, she repeats this cycle eight times. Each time, Splash feels a renewed enthusiasm and sense of commitment after finding yet another deep-sea swimming instruction book or program. And, again, each time, Splash wholeheartedly throws herself and all her energy into her efforts. Each time, Splash unfortunately also finds that she has failed yet again. And the time spent alone with chocolate ice cream increases with every failed program.

Adding to the very real fact that Splash has never been able to achieve her dream, with each subsequent failure she even begins to doubt her own abilities, her aptitude, and her resolve. As the failures mount, any time Splash begins a new swimming program, she isn't just trying to achieve her dreams; now, her self-worth is on the line. She is now also trying to prove to herself that she actually has capability and resourcefulness. And, because of this, these cycles of defeat have the unfortunate side effect of creating a new, negative self-image for Splash.

After three-plus years of trying and failing to reach her goal of being a deep-sea swimmer, Splash finally resigns herself to her fate. But because that dream will never actually go away, her day-to-day life in her fish tank now lacks the same happiness and fulfillment it once did. In order not to feel completely worthless, Splash is forced to adopt the following beliefs:

1. She will never stop wanting to be a deep-sea swimmer, but on some level she isn't worthy of being one. Deep-sea swimming must be reserved for the lucky fish that have wealthy parents, who have inside connections with the "right" fish, or who are born with the right genes.

2. The books and programs promising to teach fish to be deep-sea swimmers are all phony and nothing but alluring and hypnotically attractive lies, written to exploit the naïve dreams of little fish like her. The only thing those books really accomplish is making these "snake-oil salesfish" authors rich.

3. Because she has desired to be a deep-sea swimmer so badly and worked so hard at it, her failure makes her incredibly angry. It just isn't fair that she can't swim in the deep ocean like other fish do and she now has bitterness toward life and its lack of fairness that she'd never had in her younger days.

Have you ever felt the way Splash does? Have you, too, ever had a dream for yourself—a goal or desire that you wanted more than anything else but have been unable to achieve? If you're like most people, you have felt this way at some point in your life.

Perhaps your unrealized dream or goal involves losing unwanted weight, achieving financial freedom, finding a fulfilling career you love, being a bettor mentor to your children, or connecting with your true soul mate who loves you exactly for who you are. Maybe your dream is something very unique to you, like climbing Mount Kilimanjaro or writing the novel you've carried around in your head for the last 10 years. Or is your unrealized dream to simply, and finally, be happy in your own skin?

And, like Splash, even though you've never really been able to realize your dreams or goals as completely as you want, you've undoubtedly found that they never go away. Even repeatedly failing in your attempts to achieve them doesn't cause them to disappear, does it? Not if you're like most people. In fact, if you're like most, you've probably simply learned to justify and rationalize your inability to achieve your dreams so you don't have to live your life feeling like a complete failure. Your dreams are, after all, at the core of what it will take for you to feel fulfilled, successful, happy, and complete. It's no wonder many people begin to feel bitter about life like Splash does.

But what if I told you that every single one of those programs Splash tried was 100% capable of delivering exactly what she hoped it would? What if those authors weren't "snake oil salesfish" or phonies? What if the information they provided Splash was perfect and more than complete enough to transform her, or any fish, into a phenomenal deep-sea swimmer? As it turns out, all of these statements are true.

If that's the case, you are probably tempted to assume that the blame for Splash's failure to achieve her goals must lie squarely on her. But what if I told you that Splash not only had the perfect amount of desire to achieve her dreams, she also applied herself to those programs with more than enough willingness and effort? There was, in fact, not a single thing Splash needed to do differently. Her intentions, desires, and efforts were more than any fish would need to become a deep-sea swimmer. Additionally, there was nothing about Splash's physical or mental fitness that could have prevented her success either.

So, if all that is true about the programs Splash followed—and Splash, herself—why in the world couldn't Splash achieve her goals? And if all those things are true for you, too (and they are), why haven't you been able to more completely achieve your dreams and goals?

To solve this perplexing riddle, I need to tell you a secret about Splash. Splash lives in a very small fish tank, the type pet stores send you home with when you buy a single goldfish. Her fish tank isn't good enough for her to properly execute any of the programs she tried. Within this insufficient fish tank, no matter how much she desired it, no matter how hard Splash worked at it, and no matter how long she tried, she would never be able to achieve her dreams. Even though poor Splash will never realize this, **she** is not a failure! She would need a much better fish tank in order to put her energy and intention into action, follow an instructional program, and take her place in the deep ocean.

And now I have a secret about you to share. If you've ever felt like Splash, desiring a dream or goal intensely, finding and following expert instruction you believed in, working hard and diligently to achieve that dream or goal, yet failing to realize it, you, too, are not a failure. You, too, have a fish tank that's not good enough for you. Your fish tank is simply unsuitable for you to properly enact and execute those expert instructions you've been following. Within your current fish tank, no matter how much you desire it, no matter how hard you work at it, and no matter how long you try, you will never be able to achieve your dreams.

But, unlike Splash, you are perfectly capable of understanding that you are not a failure. You are able to see that your problem is your fish tank, not any lack of willingness, capability, resourcefulness, or even self-worth as you might have once feared. You can get a much better fish tank and now put your energy and intention into action, follow a program, and see your dreams and goals manifest before you. You can substitute the word "paradigm" for "fish tank" in this paragraph and throughout this book, because I'm going to use these two terms interchangeably throughout.

As you know, you are more fortunate than Splash because you are a sentient, self-aware animal who is capable of not only realizing you're in a fish tank in the first place, but also of being able to examine it and understand its limitations. And, better still, as a human being (unlike Splash), you can change your fish tank right now.

Also know that Splash, like anyone learning about her personal power to influence and create her life, might be tempted to respond defensively to this information. After all, with great power comes great responsibility, and, thus, this information can feel like a double-edged sword. While learning about your personal power offers you a new and clearly defined blueprint to attain many of your heretofore unattainable dreams and goals, it can also lead you to blame yourself for many of your previous bad experiences.

There is nothing to be gained by blaming yourself or beating yourself up for your previous inability to manifest your goals and I would never advocate that perspective. To the contrary, I heartily recommend that you waste no energy trying to blame yourself for your prior failings. Instead my message to Splash (and to you) is very strong: in a sense, you are not responsible for your past experiences - since they occurred prior to learning about your personal power. And my follow-up directive is simple: rather than blaming yourself for your painful past, focus, instead, on making a positive difference in your life experiences from this point forward. You are now able to take responsibility for your life experiences, just for today, for as long as you live.

But allow me to go a step further in my recommendations and directives. Not only should you not blame yourself for your previous failings, you should also not expect perfection from this point forward. When you have a bad experience, or fail to create a desire result, that does not mean you "wanted" that outcome and, thus, are further to blame. That is too harsh a self-evaluation; you should be a much gentler taskmaster towards yourself as you learn to harness and fully utilize your inherent creative power. You will make mistakes and you will also experience unwanted results without any discernible cause. In fact, later, I'll explain why this is not only to be expected, but actually to be celebrated. For now, pay attention solely to your improving power to influence and create a more desirable reality and focus on progress, not perfection, as your ability to consciously align your life experiences with your personal dreams and goals grows.

That's exactly what this book teaches you to do. By providing you with new paradigms from the more accurate science of the second scientific revolution, quantum physics, you will now ditch that old goldfish tank and move into an aquarium.

Chapter Three: How You Got that Little Goldfish Tank in the First Place

"Taken over the centuries, scientific ideas have exerted a force on our civilization fully as great as the more tangible practical applications of scientific research."

Bernard Cohen
Science Historian

Before we move you into your spacious new aquarium, let's look at how you got your current, not-good-enough fish tank in the first place. After all, one hundred years ago it was thought to be the best tank possible. What the first scientific revolution did was not only resolve the mysteries of the universe (or so we thought, of course), but it also raised people out of the superstitious and fearful fish tanks in which the Western world's lack of accurate scientific understanding held them. You see, prior to the first scientific revolution, relatively everyone in the Western world believed the following scientific "facts":

* All of existence was a moment-to-moment, renewable miracle, and God's divine power was the one and only cause or explanation for any of it.

* There were only four elements on Earth, and all things here were made of them: air, fire, earth, and water.

* Fire and air, being lightweight, naturally traveled upward, above the Earth, and combined to form a fifth element called aether.

* Everything not on the Earth (stars, planets, moon, etc.) was made of aether.

* The Earth was the center of the universe; the Sun and the planets revolved around the Earth in epicycles.

* The one and only cause of all planetary motion was God's divine power.

*And, of course, the Earth was flat.

And even though I referred to the preceding as "scientific" facts, Western scholars didn't practice science as we know it today. People pursued scientific knowledge within the scope of religious study, and scientific endeavors were seen purely as attempts to glorify God and to verify religious doctrine. (I'm not belittling religious faith here; many people in the 21st century still believe in God and God's power, but we also acknowledge science as a scholarly discipline not tied to religion.)

Imagine the frightening fish tanks the people of the Western world lived in. Even though it may currently be difficult for you to achieve some of your dreams or goals, imagine trying to do so in such little fish tanks. Before the scientific revolution was fully integrated into the world, even the most learned, educated, and successful people of Western civilization considered the preceding list of "facts" to be absolute truths, and people's fish tanks were predicated upon beliefs culled from these "facts." Within their fish tanks, the following strange practices and beliefs were commonplace:

* People wrapped urine-soaked hose around their neck to fight off colds.

* People thought that the planets moved around in the "universal aether" because they were being pushed by angels.

* Surgeons carved holes in skulls to cure migraines, seizures, and mental illness.

* Beaver testicles were ground up and mixed with alcohol as a female contraceptive.

* Mercury, a deadly poison, was applied externally to cure wounds and consumed internally to cure a wide variety of ailments such as constipation.

* People believed that bad smells and malodorous vapors caused illness.

* Women rubbed puppy urine on their faces as a beauty treatment (and even brushed their teeth with it).

*You would fall off the edge of the world if you sailed a boat too far into the ocean.

* Farmers believed that having sexual intercourse under an evergreen tree produced abundant and fertile harvests.

Although we can probably find some farmers who wouldn't mind reviving that last one, can you imagine living within the paradigms these people did? If you encountered a civilization still living like this today, you would consider them in need of immediate and urgent help. And you'd be correct. For people living in the Western world of the 16th century, life was a daily struggle of trying to somehow please God to gain His favor so you might possibly avoid debilitating disease, extreme poverty, near starvation, and physical hardship. Since there was no real scientific understanding of how the natural world operated, the Western world's fish tanks had no provision for the vast majority of people to live truly healthy, successful lives.

But that help did finally come to the Western world in the form of the first scientific revolution. The science of Newton uncovered the mysteries of the physical world and provided real (yet, we now know, inaccurate) answers about how our universe functioned. And the fish tanks of the Western world changed in tandem with the landmark scientific achievements of the first scientific revolution. Yet, as amazing as it might sound, people will someday look back on the fish tanks which came from the first scientific revolution (the very ones you've been living in) and, even though they are incredibly more accurate and helpful than the ones they replaced, have the same fascination at our scientific ignorance and our superstitious habits.

Future humans will read about our era and see that we were almost as in need of immediate and urgent help as the people of 16th century were. Luckily, you will be able to tell these people (because your head will probably still be alive in a cryogenic chamber of some sort), "I could see the handwriting on the wall back in 2012 and adopted the new paradigms of the second scientific revolution during those primitive times." And won't you feel smart?

Let's revisit the four fundamental things the science of the first scientific revolution revealed so we can then look at the paradigms that were created by each of them.

1. Each "thing" is made of smaller parts with predictable functions. This gave rise to the paradigm of mechanism.

2. For every action, there is an equal and opposite reaction. This gave rise to the paradigm we call determinism.

3. The observer and the observed are two separate things. This gave rise to the paradigm of separateness.

4. Things occur in a logical, linear fashion. This gave rise to the paradigm of logical outcomes.

The machine paradigm creates a fish tank where everything in our world can be broken down into smaller units. These smaller units not only have jobs that make the larger unit function properly, but they also have predictable roles when performing their jobs. The smaller parts can be easily identified. When the larger unit is malfunctioning, in this fish tank you always look for the smaller part that is not doing its job properly and either fix it or replace it. This paradigm has us looking at everything in the universe as if it's an old-fashioned clock with moving parts.

The determinism paradigm creates a fish tank where action is the most important thing we can do if we want anything to change. Action becomes the only force for causing a desired response. And, if we are experiencing unwanted results, we always identify one of two things: Either we find the action we should be taking to get the desired results and then start doing it, or we find the action we shouldn't be taking which is keeping the desired results from materializing and then stop doing it. This paradigm has us looking at everything in the universe as needing our physical intervention if we want different results than we're experiencing.

The separateness paradigm creates a fish tank where whatever or whoever we are observing is an entirely distinct and estranged object from us. We expect to be able to tinker and experiment with things in the world because they are separate from us. In this paradigm, when we want to observe something (or someone) we are free to do so from a detached distance (both literally and metaphorically), evaluating what we observe as a completely separate entity who has no influence over the behavior of what she is observing. This paradigm has us looking at everything in the universe as if we can observe behaviors like a psychologist watching a test subject through a one-way mirror.

The logical outcomes paradigm creates a fish tank where we can always use logic to determine how to affect a desired outcome. Once we determine the outcome we desire and learn the steps it takes to achieve that outcome, all we need to do is take those steps. Then, we can expect reliable results. Additionally, if we are experiencing an undesirable outcome, we can learn the steps necessary for a desirable one, and then examine which of the steps in the undesirable outcome was out of order or incorrect. Once identified, we can then correct the undesired outcome by replacing the incorrect step with the correct one. This paradigm has us looking at everything in the universe as being doable or attainable if we simply learn the proper process for its achievement and enact that process.

Whether or not the labels for those four paradigms were already familiar to you, I know the descriptions of them are because they are descriptions of your current fish tanks. Those four paradigms became the predominant fish tanks for citizens of the Western world after the first scientific revolution when great minds applied them to other fields and disciplines. And these fish tanks are still in use today simply because the great thinkers of the 21st century are not yet writing about the new paradigms from quantum physics. And, no, as highly as I regard myself and as much as I love and believe in this book, I won't give myself the title "great thinker of the 21st century." Of course, if you want to call me that after reading this book, send me an email and I'll name my next pet after you (sorry…I'm done having children).

To illustrate how great thinkers used these paradigms from the first scientific revolution to create new fish tanks for the Western world, let's look at one example: Freud. Before I draw the ire of mental health professionals reading this book, please understand that I fully realize that many of Freud's theories are no longer regarded with primacy within that community. I cite him simply because he used paradigms from the first scientific revolution to completely alter a discipline and create new fish tanks for all of us.

When Freud became a psychiatrist in the late 19th century, mental illness was still being treated purely medically. A patient with neurosis, for example, was treated by the same principles as a patient with a broken arm. She was treated through physical means. For example, it was thought that stimulation of the sinuses would cure mental illness, so cocaine was used to stimulate the sinuses of mentally ill patients. Others underwent cranial surgery to treat their mental illness.

Freud used the classical physics paradigm of determinism to create an entirely new discipline called psychotherapy. Determinism states that you can always find out why something went wrong by tracing backwards logically, through the line of actions that caused the thing, and identifying the mistaken or incorrect action. Determinism tells us that we can then correct the thing that went wrong by correcting the mistake that led to it. Freud surmised that if a patient had a mental disorder, he could lead that patient on an examination of her past, discover the source of her mental distress, and "fix" that source of her mental distress (her mental wound) through talk therapy. While Freud's central theme of sex as the primary source of mental distress has since been largely discarded, his theory of psychoanalysis still forms the basis for the treatment of mental illness and the modern Western disciplines of psychology and psychiatry.

Not only was Freud completely influenced by the classical physics paradigm of determinism, he would not even have been able to formulate the treatment without having that paradigm in place. Bear in mind that the treatment of mental illness was completely a physical process before Freud's work and, in fact, his theories were openly ridiculed by his psychiatric peers until time (and his persistence) overcame the psychiatric community's resistance to such radical notions as past experiences or behavior being a cause of mental distress. Without this paradigm's existence, which wouldn't have happened without the science of the first scientific revolution, Freud would have had no frame of reference for such a theory; he needed a better fish tank to have ever envisioned his theories.

Ironically, Freud's theories were inspired by the work of Darwin, who previously used determinism to create an entirely new discipline, evolutionary biology. Darwin proposed that evolution determined animal behavior, which gave Freud the idea that human behavior could be determined by human evolution (in this case, childhood development). So, while there is no clear record of Freud crediting the paradigm of determinism from the science of the first scientific revolution for inspiring his theories, he was most certainly influenced by one of his fellow great thinker's use of this classical physics paradigm.

The paradigms of mechanism, determinism, separateness, and logical outcomes were all created from classical physics, the science of the first scientific revolution. They represented paradigm shifts away from the dark, inadequate fish tanks of the Western world prior to the 16th century. Our modern methods of government, business, education, medicine, philosophy, parenting, finances, relationships, and many other fields are all the byproducts of these paradigms. I could write an entire book describing how an endless array of great thinkers applied these paradigms to their fields and disciplines to create better fish tanks for every person living in Western civilization from the 16th century until today.

Yet, the science of the first scientific revolution has been supplanted by the new, more accurate science of quantum physics. In fact, quantum physics is so much more precise and reliable that it has caused a second scientific revolution. Those changes are already underway, and you'll soon be participating in them.

Chapter Four: Quantum Physics and New Fish Tanks for Everyone

"If anybody says he can think about quantum physics without getting giddy, that only shows he has not understood the first thing about them."

Niels Bohr
Physicist
Nobel Prize Winner

I've written that the second scientific revolution, quantum physics, has provided us with amazingly accurate, new scientific knowledge. Quantum physics is causing scientists to reform everything they thought they knew about how our universe works. Much of what quantum physics teaches us, in fact, is the polar opposite of what we once thought we knew about our universe. What follows are four of the basic tenants of the second scientific revolution:

* All matter is made up of organic, or unified, wholes that are often greater than the sum of their parts. This concept is called holism, and it is the polar opposite of the machine metaphor of the first scientific revolution.

* There is not necessarily a relationship between cause and effect. Action is not always caused by another force exerting itself.

* The observer and the observed cannot be separated. The observer's observation and expectations literally become a part of what is being observed. In fact, the observer and the observed may be said to be two different perspectives of the same thing.

* Systems are not linear. Systems are equations whose effects are not proportional to their causes. There is a lack of logical sequence, correlation, or cohesion found in the universe where we once thought that everything was neatly and logically ordered.

You probably noticed immediately that each one of these four principles is ordered to correspond with the scientific "fact" from the first scientific revolution that it has supplanted. Whether or not you are able to wrap your head around those four principles on your first read, I'm sure you can recognize that they actually tell us that what we previously believed to be true about how our universe works is largely false. And that is a great starting point because it allows you to take the next logical step in acquiring your better fish tanks: the paradigms, or fish tanks, from the first scientific revolution are also largely false.

Before we examine the new fish tanks that quantum physics provides us, let's take a moment to address something important. Quantum physics governs the world of microscopic (subatomic) particles and macroscopic (immense) bodies in our universe, while classical physics is the science that governs the universe we can see with our naked eyes. The principals of classical physics are still useful in our day-to-day lives.

For example, classical physics makes it possible for us to design reliable airplanes. And some have argued that, because classical physics is still useful, the paradigms from it should still be adhered to.

My first response to this argument is to agree that the paradigms from classical physics are obviously huge improvements over the paradigms they replaced. As everyone has experienced, our world functions pretty darn well using these paradigms, and modern Western people are largely free from the rampant disease, poverty, starvation, and physical hardship people suffered before their creation (although many parts of our world still do experience these conditions on a daily basis). Yet, I will counter that Western people are still in need of better fish tanks, further personal evolution, if you will, which can easily be seen through our continual quest for not only more personal health, success, efficacy, and ease of being, but also in the ongoing search for fulfilling personal happiness and satisfaction. The very fact that you are reading this book speaks clearly to the self-evident fact that, although your life is far better than a 15th century European's was, you are still not satisfied with your current fish tank. And why should you be satisfied when your inner knowing correctly tells you that better ways of achieving your goals and dreams, of being personally fulfilled, must exist?

My second response is that quantum science actually does govern the world we see with our naked eye. It is not relegated to the micro and macroscopic parts of our universe. Intuitively you can discern that, if everything in the material world is made of microscopic particles, the larger objects of the material world must adhere to the properties of those particles that form them.

Third, quantum physics does govern the world visible to our naked eye just as it governs the micro and macroscopic, and it can be illustrated using our planet. You know that our planet is a globe, which is a fact that can be verified with your eyes simply by looking at photographs of it from outer space. But when you walk out your front door, do you see a round Earth? Of course not. You see a flat Earth, and there is no perspective on our Earth from which you can see its roundedness with your naked eye. This is because of your tiny size relative to the size of the Earth—your relative perspective of it. You are too small to have the perspective to see the Earth as a globe unless you leave it and look down from space. In this manner, perspective also alters your ability to see quantum effects with your naked eye in various ways. Yet, just as you know the Earth is round even when it looks flat from your perspective, you can rest assured that quantum physics is governing the behavior of the entire material world even when it still looks like a classical physics world to the naked eye.

Finally, there is one fundamental quality of microscopic particles, about which you'll learn more later, that reveals exactly why the material world, visible with your naked eye, almost always appears to be one governed by the old science of classical physics: Microscopic particles are not actually particles at all. Subatomic particles, strange as this might sound, are not tangible, physical objects. They are merely possibilities. Until they are manifest into concrete material objects (which occurs when they are observed), subatomic particles exist in a state of pure potential; they are neither particle nor wave and are completely unformed. The act of observing a subatomic particle is what makes it take a definite form and, once they take a concrete form (we call observed particles that have taken a definite form a "localized time-space event"), they no longer exhibit quantum properties visible to your naked eye. And, since everything you see with your naked eye is a localized time-space event, until recently it has been largely impossible to observe quantum effects on an everyday level. Yet, even when they are a localized time-space event, the subatomic particles that comprise every material object still retain their quantum properties and abilities.

Quantum effects are now actually being seen in objects visible to the naked eye. Buckyballs, relatively huge molecules made of carbon atoms, and even small diamonds have demonstrated quantum effects on a less than microscopic level. And, recently, physicists Andrew Cleland and Aaron O'Connell (in two separate experiments) created objects, viewable to the naked eye, that each demonstrates quantum effects we can see. Although the term "see" is relative, because it's probably more accurate to say that their quantum effects can be measured, this is still an amazing development considering the challenges that subatomic particles pose to physicists.

What follows is a brief reprise of each of quantum physics' four main principles, the new fish tank we now have because of it, and the old fish tank it replaces:

* All matter is made up of unified wholes that are often greater than the sum of their parts. This gives rise to the new paradigm of holism and replaces the old paradigm of mechanism.

* There is not necessarily a relationship between cause and effect. This gives rise to the new paradigm of unity and replaces the old paradigm of determinism.

* The observer and the observed cannot be separated. This gives rise to the new paradigm of entanglement and replaces the old paradigm of separateness.

* Systems are not linear. This gives rise to the new paradigm of nonlinearity and replaces the old paradigm of logical outcomes.

The titles I've given these paradigms are mine, so they may differ from ones you've read previously. And don't worry if any of these terms sound foreign to you. The label of each new paradigm is not as important as the new, better fish tank it provides for you. Each of these new fish tanks is just as much an improvement over the reasons you've always done things the way you've done them as the paradigms of the first scientific revolution were for people in the Western world after the 16th century. I'll explain each of these new fish tanks in greater detail now. And, after discussing each of them, I'll provide a new unified, combined paradigm that will allow you to begin using these fish tanks right now, on a daily basis, to improve your life and achieve your dreams and goals.

Isn't it interesting to note that your great-grandchildren will probably some day marvel at the list of archaic beliefs we held in the 20th century? Similar to your dismayed reaction to the pre-classical physics' beliefs I listed in Chapter 3, our descendents will one day say, "Can you believe that people used to believe that…"

"…focusing almost entirely upon their actions was the most important component for any change they wanted to make, such as having a fit, trim body?"

"…they were a detached observer of life and that their own personal expectations weren't just as much a part of the outcomes as the things they were observing, as if they had no influence over the results?"

"…they could predictably alter their results of any undertaking by fixing, or tinkering with, the smaller components of a larger system, as if larger systems behaved like the workings of a clock?"

"…by using logic, they could expect and enjoy reliable and consistent outcomes, as if the steps they took to produce those intended results inherently led to just that one outcome?"

For the sake of avoiding confusion, before continuing I want to note that there are a few terms I'll keep using interchangeably. You already know that I'm using the terms "fish tank" and "paradigm" interchangeably. Additionally, the terms "classical physics" and "the first scientific revolution" are used interchangeably. And, finally, I will use the terms "quantum physics" and "the second scientific revolution" interchangeably. Now, any time you see any of these different words, you will know what I'm writing about.

Chapter Five: The New Fish Tank of Holism

"In the new pattern of thought we do not assume any longer the detached observer, occurring in the idealizations of this classical type of theory, but an observer who by his indeterminable effects creates a new situation, theoretically described as a new state of the observed system."

Wolfgang Pauli
Physicist
Nobel Prize Winner

The first new fish tank we'll examine is holism. Quantum physics tell us that larger objects and systems are not machines composed of smaller parts with predictable functions working collectively to serve and further the larger entity—which is the fish tank of mechanism. The second scientific revolution teaches us that it is more accurate to replace the machine paradigm with the holistic paradigm. Viewing larger objects and systems (such as your body) through the holistic paradigm will open doors to personal success that had previously remained locked for you.

The machine paradigm says that a complex system can be explained by reducing it to its smallest fundamental parts. Quantum physics shows us, however, that this is not true. Systems, we've learned, cannot be defined so simply. In the machine paradigm, systems are fixed; that is, they remain the same in all situations. You don't need the second scientific revolution to know, intuitively, that this metaphor has too many limitations when applied to our world. Something as basic as your state of being is context dependent. You have many sides and facets to your character that are drawn out by different circumstances or associations.

Sometimes a driver cutting you off in traffic will elicit a very angry response from you, while at other times it doesn't bother you the slightest bit. If the machine paradigm were truly most accurate, you would have the same response to being cut off in traffic every time.

The machine paradigm is exact and stresses a "black or white," "either/or" vision that does not work best for us. This old paradigm, for example, offers no real role for free will. Any system is thought of as a machine whose parts are powered by internal and external forces beyond your scope or control. For example, even subconscious influences from your childhood are thought to cause effects in your current adult life. Whether you currently believe this is true or not, it is an example of the machine paradigm in action, and it is too limiting.

The second scientific revolution tells us that systems aren't modeled after a machine. Instead, they're holistic. While the machine paradigm would have us deconstruct our systems (bodies, minds, organizations, groups, etc.), the holistic paradigm asks us to look at these entities as whole systems to better understand them. Instead of breaking down larger systems into smaller parts, we look at the entire system and see how its different components, often greater than the aggregate, interact and cooperate to form a whole.

In fact, you should think of your physical body not as a machine, but as a collection of "free agents," or whole, independent systems, just as vital individually as they are when taken as a collective (the "collective" being, of course, "you" in your entirety). These systems that make up "you" are cooperating for no known reason, but there is ample evidence that they each have their own agenda and independent actions, which are usually carried out below our level of consciousness and awareness. Some of them, such as our immune system, even offer evidence that they may have a consciousness separate from the larger "you"!

For example, when was the last time you commanded your heart to beat or your lungs to breath or your eyelids to blink? When was the last time you consciously and actively coordinated the countless nerves, muscles, tendons, etc., to work in intricate precision, allowing you to walk across the room? When did you last specifically coordinate the perfect firing of electricity through neurons across your brain's hemispheres to recall a childhood memory or your neighbor's phone number?

The machine metaphor has led you to think of yourself as a machine with smaller parts and predictable functions. I hope you're realizing that this is just not so. But if you still maintain doubt or wish to cling to the old paradigm, perhaps you could benefit from what might be a shocking revelation. What follows is a true story that shows you just how independently your systems actually operate and just how much those systems' motives can sometimes trump the greater functioning of the larger system that is your body.

In the early 1990s, Dr. Candice Pert, while serving as the chief molecular biologist for the National Institutes of Health, made an amazing discovery that beautifully illustrates the concept of holism in our bodies. As opposed to a machine, where all the smaller parts' "job" is to work for the greater functions of the larger entity, Dr. Pert found amazing evidence that your body is actually a unified whole (just as the second scientific revolution predicts).

Amazing as it sounds, Dr. Pert discovered that your thoughts are real, physical things. Your thoughts, it turns out, aren't fluffy, ethereal stuff; they are tangible objects. Here's how it works.

Every thought you have, Dr. Pert found, has a unique neuropeptide associated with it, and your body, in turn, produces that unique neuropeptide every time you experience that particular thought (and the emotion associated with it). A neuropeptide is a simple, protein-based amino acid and is produced by your hypothalamus, a "control center" at the base of your brain.

Every time you have a thought, your hypothalamus "translates" that thought into billions of neuropeptides that are uniquely associated with the emotion you are experiencing because of your thought. And then your bloodstream is flooded with billions of the unique neuropeptides associated with the emotion you have just been experiencing. Your thought, translated into a neuropeptide, literally becomes a molecular messenger of emotion.

When in your bloodstream, these neuropeptides are physically assimilated by your body's cells. The neuropeptides conjoin with your cells by inserting themselves into a special receptacle on each cell's membrane—just like a key fitting into a keyhole. Each neuropeptide receptacle on a cell's membrane is specifically designed to fit just that one particular peptide and no other. So once that neuropeptide finds the right receptacle on the cell membrane, that amino acid is absorbed into the cell.

Over time, Dr. Pert found, your cells develop more and more unique receptacles on their membranes to capture the neuropeptides to which they are most often exposed. And she also found that, over time, your cells begin to crave the neuropeptides to which they are most often exposed (and have built the unique receptacles to receive). In fact, Dr. Pert found that your cells become so accustomed to the unique neuropeptides to which they are most often exposed that they cover their membranes with nothing but receptacles for those neuropeptides. Actually shutting down other vital functions, your cells become nothing but vessels to ingest the unique neuropeptides they predominantly experience.

So your cells start "telling" your hypothalamus to produce these particular neuropeptides because they have developed an actual physical need for them. Think of a person who becomes physically addicted to a chemical, abandoning family, jobs, friends, and personal well-being to chase the drug, and you've got a reasonable facsimile of what happens to your cells.

One of the most sobering aspects of Dr. Pert's findings, you're probably realizing, is that the only way your hypothalamus can produce the neuropeptides that your cells are now physically addicted to is for you to experience the emotions that will create them. And the only way your brain can experience the emotions necessary to create those neuropeptides is for it to see and experience a physical reality that will elicit those emotions.

So if you've spent years thinking, "People don't like me," "I'm useless," and "I can't do that," you've inadvertently addicted the cells of your body, on a physical level, to the neuropeptides that your hypothalamus creates when you experience the emotions associated with those messages of self-doubt. Your cells have built billions of unique receptacles for each unique neuropeptide you've predominantly exposed them to (through your emotional states). And your cells are now asking for them all day, every day. In this manner, your cells are, literally, dictating what you experience because they are controlling your emotional states. Your body may actually be physically addicted to certain emotional states, even if these emotional states are painful or unwanted by your conscious awareness.

If you have doubts about this information, by the way, I encourage you to read Dr. Pert's research to learn just how real and verifiable this process is. (Candace Pert, *Molecules of Emotion*, New York: Scribner, 2010)

Not only are you not in charge of this process, chances are you had no idea this was even going on. Can you begin to see, through this example, that your cells are not smaller parts of a larger machine whose "job" is to serve the larger entity (your body)? Don't you agree that it's much more accurate to say that your cells, like the rest of your body, are organic wholes with independent agendas that are greater than the sum of their parts? Your cells act like independent entities, not gears in a clock.

If your cells are calling the shots, forcing your brain to see and experience a world that will produce the emotions to which they've become addicted, isn't it easy to see that the machine paradigm in regards to your body is inaccurate? Your body's "parts" have not been behaving in reliable and predictable fashions, performing their "job" to make the larger "machine" functions the way you'd most want it to, have they?

All this activity has been happening in your body without your knowledge or your consent. In fact, research on neuropeptides shows that your immune system produces its own peptides—which suggests that your immune system may have its own independent consciousness. Isn't it easy to see that, as the holistic paradigm shows, your body's smaller systems can often be called, individually, greater than the larger system they were supposed to be "serving" (under the old machine paradigm)?

The fish tank of holism doesn't mean that you should no longer count on a system's components helping the functioning of the larger entity.

Yet it does free you from the unrealistic expectations of precise responses from those components when you "tinker" with them to make the larger system function better. Additionally, you can release some of the frustration and self-blame you may have felt when larger systems, such as your body, have not responded as you'd expected to corrective actions or intended improvements.

Chapter Six: The New Fish Tank of Unity

"From the quantum mechanical perspective, to measure the position of an electron is not to find out where it is but to cause it to be somewhere."

Louisa Gilder
Science Author

The next new fish tank from quantum physics is called unity, and it replaces the action-based paradigm of the first scientific revolution with one that more accurately reflects the way our universe really operates. Science now tells us that your actions are, quite literally, not the most important component for any event or circumstance, as classical physics taught us.

The action-based paradigm stressed that every response or outcome in our universe can be explained by finding the thing that has exerted itself upon that which moved or changed. Forces such as gravity, momentum, mass in motion, or, simply, someone or something pushing are always responsible for any movement or change. This is a logical explanation for movement and not only jibes with our common sense but also meets the "naked eye" test. In fact, Newton considered the idea of anything contrary to the action-based paradigm to be completely irrational and utter nonsense.

The action-based paradigm is also applied to non-physical movement such as your state of mind, your decisions, political movements, business, and philosophy. If, for example, you have a problem in your life, you have been taught that non-physical forces may be just as responsible as physical ones. In the action-based paradigm, forces such as your upbringing, social expectations, popular culture, and the way you were parented as a child are all thought to be responsible for your problem. Once again, this is logical to us and is generally accepted because it appeals to our common sense and what we've been taught.

But you don't even need the second scientific revolution to know, intuitively, that the second part of this metaphor has too many limitations when applied to our universe. On a personal level, you know your life is certainly context dependent. You have seen too many examples of people who are not affected by the same issues to know that a force applied to you will not always produce a predictable result.

For example, you are undoubtedly aware of people who grew up very poor, in a household where money and resources were lacking, yet who are now financially successful. In the realm of physical forces exerting themselves, you are also probably aware of people who don't seem to work as hard at their jobs as you, yet who experience greater financial reward. Whether or not these examples apply to you, I hope you can see that the same forces, when applied to different people in different situations, do not usually produce predictable, reliable, or consistent results.

The unity paradigm represents a shift away from looking at the material world (outside of you) as what is causing you to feel a certain way or experience certain results in your life. The science of the second scientific revolution shows us that the outside world is created by one's inside world, not the other way around. Your internal energy creates the material world outside of you. Embracing this paradigm, as weird as it may sound to you right now, is as logical a scientific "next step" for humanity as embracing the Earth's revolution around the sun was for a person in the 17th century.

When you study the science of the second scientific revolution, you will learn that the entire universe is actually an unformed field of energy called the quantum field. The quantum field is a non-local and unbounded energy field representing all possibilities because it has no definite form (yet). In layman's terms, it is everywhere all at once, it is endless and uncontained, and it can become, literally, anything. In other words, the quantum field is a mass of energy with the potential to form anything: you, me, trees, clouds, automobiles, toy soldiers, dental floss, planets, whales, etc. (literally, everything you see and encounter in the material world).

All physical matter in the universe is manifested from the quantum field. This field waits in a state of infinite possibility for you to manifest the material world from it—which you do, either deliberately or accidentally, every second of every day you're alive. The material world does not pre-exist, awaiting your observation; you create the material world, through your observations, on a moment-by-moment basis.

The scientific explanation for this is that subatomic particles exist in a state of mere potential until they are observed. Strange as it sounds, your observation creates electrons' state, form, and location. Prior to your observation of them, subatomic particles have merely the *potential* to become something material and concrete.

Yes, the second scientific revolution has clearly determined that you have created, from the quantum field, all that you see and experience in this physical universe. You created everything you now see. It wasn't here waiting for you to discover it. Stop and look around your room right now. Every single thing you see and experience has been created by you from the quantum field. Even though it sounds like science fiction, it's not; if you weren't here to observe, those material objects wouldn't exist.

In fact, the most important quantum physics experiment (so important that Nobel Prize-winning physicist Richard Feynman called it "the only thing you need to know about quantum physics") shows us very clearly that you literally create the material world.

The experiment is called the double-slit experiment, and it uses an electron gun to fire particles at a far wall through two slits. The gist of this experiment is that the particles fired through the double slits always take the form they are expected to take. The observation of the observer is what dictates the electron's form (whether wave or particle). And, stranger still, the electrons actually have no form until they are observed. They do not preexist in any certain form, waiting to be observed. The act of observing is what prompts them to take on any form at all! (There are volumes of written material about the double-slit experiment, by the way, if you'd like to read about it in more detail.)

Another way of framing this new paradigm is to think of it this way: The unity paradigm tells us we must switch our perspective from bottom-up to top-down. The old science said that the material world existed irrespective of you, the observer. Creation was a bottom-up process. The material world existed in a predetermined state, awaiting your discovery. The new, more accurate science of quantum physics tells us just the opposite. The material world is actually created by you, through your discovery or observations. Creation, it turns out, is a top-down process. The building blocks of all material things exist in a state of mere unrealized potential until you (the observer) turn your attention to them and command them to take a concrete and final form.

From this perhaps bizarre-sounding science of the second scientific revolution, we can construct a much more accurate, unity paradigm to replace the outdated action-based one. If you're not yet convinced that your actions are almost irrelevant when compared to the importance of your expectations, you soon will be.

Quantum physics shows us that we create our material world from the quantum field through our observations. Since the quantum field has the potential to become, literally, anything, it responds to our observations to know what to materialize as. In other words, you see and experience exactly what you expect to see and experience. For example, you expected to see the chair you sat in when you entered the room, so it was waiting for you—created for you from the quantum field. You expected to experience the lamp lighting the room so you could read, so the lamp was waiting for you—also created for you from the quantum field. And so it is with every single thing you encounter, every experience you have, every moment of every day.

The unity paradigm tells us that the physical world is not what is most "real" in the sense that it is completely subjective and created solely through your observations. Your energy is the source of the "outer" world that we have erroneously been led to believe is preexisting, concrete, and unchanging. While you can see, touch, smell, and hear the physical world, it seems to be the most "real." But, since it is your inner energy that creates the physical world, isn't it more accurate to say that your inner energy is actually much more real than the physical world itself? And, since we now know this, you can embrace the unity between you and the material world you are creating right now.

Dr. Deepak Chopra talks about Dr. Wilder Penfield, a famous Canadian neurosurgeon whose research discovered the brain's sensory and motor cortex, among other things. During his studies of the motor cortex, having found the area of our brain where decisions are carried out, Penfield was said to have been excited by the prospect of one day finding the area of our brain where decisions are made. It may surprise you to learn that Penfield never found that part of our brain—because there is no part of our brain where decisions are made.

In fact, there is no part of your physical body where decisions are made. Your body, and every part of it, is an elegant tool, perfect for executing decisions but not for making them. Yet you know beyond a shadow of a doubt that you are making decisions every day. So who is making those decisions if it's not your physical body? The only possible answer must be that there is a non-physical "you" and, since this energy is making your decisions, this non-physical energy is much more "you" than your body is.

The unity paradigm does not tell us that your actions are irrelevant. To the contrary, actions will always be an important part of the physical universe and for making changes in it. What the unity paradigm does, however, is set you free from relying solely upon your actions as your primary source of change. Essentially, you can stop beating yourself up for taking the seeming "wrong actions" when you don't find the success you are looking for or the results you desire. And you can also stop your continual search for that one magical set of actions that will finally deliver the results you've wanted, because there is no such thing.

Chapter Seven: The New Fish Tank of Entanglement

"Subject and object are only one. The barrier between them cannot be said to have broken down as a result of recent experience in the physical sciences, for this barrier does not exist."

Erwin Schrodinger
Physicist
Nobel Prize Winner

Now let's discuss our next new paradigm, entanglement. Quantum physics shows us that the observer and that which she is observing are not actually two separate things. They are simply two unique perspectives of the same thing. Classical physics had previously, and erroneously, taught that the observer and the observed are two independent entities. And the ramifications of this rule of classical physics had deep implications for the modern world in which we live. The lack of separation shown through quantum physics is, in fact, a complete departure from the paradigm of separateness the world adopted after the first scientific revolution.

When the first scientific revolution created the paradigm of separateness, it quickly became part of almost every field and discipline in the modern world. It won't be difficult to see just how pervasive this paradigm is for you. Separateness tells you that you can always examine anything from "afar," removed from the outcome, and that you can always experiment with or "tinker" with outcomes by adjusting variables. Think of the scientist who conducts an experiment by adding agents to a solution and then recording the results, or a psychologist who watches her test subjects while hidden from their view and cataloging the data.

To see this paradigm in our modern world is easy, and there are actually far too many examples to list them all. Let's take a look at but one: separateness in the modern weight loss industry. Our modern weight loss industry relies heavily (perhaps completely) upon separateness.

If you have unwanted weight, after all, you are treated like a test subject in an experiment; you are told to zero in on the cause of your problem so you can fix it. Eating the wrong foods? That's an "easy fix." Simply correct your diet and your experiment will become successful. Doing the wrong (or not enough) exercises? Another "easy fix" and your experiment will be back on track. Perhaps you have experienced emotional trauma during childhood and you're currently abusing food to cover up negative feelings? You can "fix" that through a therapeutic process and get the results you want from your experiment. Can you think of a weight loss program (other than my book, *Why Quantum Physicists Don't Get Fat*) that doesn't treat you and your body like test subjects that will respond predictably to such tinkering?

And while you may not immediately find the separateness paradigm to be incorrect (because you grew up being taught this paradigm), ask yourself if this fish tank is giving you the results you truly desire. Even if you aren't experiencing problems with unwanted weight, I can tell you with assurance that this fish tank is not working for the majority of Americans. Statistics from the U.S. Food and Drug Administration, Marketdata, and the Centers for Disease Control and Prevention show we are spending over $60 billion a year on weight loss, yet the country's obesity rate balloons. And it's difficult to make the case that this is due to simple lack of will power. After all, spending so much on weight loss plans indicates a huge desire to lose weight.

Even if you are successful at keeping your desired weight, though, I'm still quite sure of two things. One, you wouldn't turn down an opportunity to add even greater success and happiness to your life by using the new fish tank of entanglement. Two, you can easily see that losing weight is a massive challenge for millions of Americans who obviously desire improvements enough to spend billions on it, yet who are unsuccessful because they're still relying on the old paradigm of separateness. Isn't it plain to see that the limitations of separateness are presenting huge roadblocks for our modern world?

The instructions provided to us by the modern weight loss industry are very simple and straightforward: Eat less and exercise more. How hard could it be to comprehend those instructions and follow them? I propose that the problem lies not in the instructions themselves but in the old fish tanks we inhabit.

Remember poor little Splash's experiences? I propose it's time to build a better fish tank—a fish tank where the simple instructions for weight loss can be fully utilized and made to work as we expect they ought to. This new fish tank, or paradigm, of entanglement from the second scientific revolution is probably going to be a rather strange concept given your current "old science" paradigms. In quantum physics, entanglement happens when two particles, having once been in physical proximity to each other, are separated—even by astronomical distances. These particles somehow remain connected to one another in terms of their movement and position. And entanglement occurs not just with subatomic particles, but even with "large" particles like buckyballs and small diamonds.

When particles are entangled, the movement or position of one of them will always create a corresponding opposite movement in the other. What makes this discovery remarkable is that this connection remains even when these particles are very far away from one another. So if a scientist in Newark, New Jersey, spins one of two entangled particles clockwise, the other entangled particle, even if it's located on Pluto, will immediately begin to spin in a counter-clockwise direction. There is no clear answer to why particles retain this connection, nor is there a ready answer to solve the mystery of how the information is traversing even immense distances instantaneously, traveling faster than the speed of light. All we can say with certainty is that we now know this effect is very real and can be reliably duplicated by physicists.

And hold on to your seat, because it gets even stranger. Recent quantum experiments have demonstrated something called "delayed-choice entanglement swapping." Delayed-choice entanglement swapping shows us that information between entangled particles can actually travel backward in time. Two pairs of particles (four total particles, in two pairs, each entangled to its mate) are separated into three locations. One of the two paired particles is in Louisville, Kentucky; one of the other paired particles is in Los Angeles, California; and the remaining two (each entangled with its pair, which remains in either Louisville or Los Angeles) are in Beijing, China. If the scientist in Beijing chooses to entangle the pair she has (or doesn't choose to entangle them), the particles in Louisville and Los Angeles will have correlated polarizations even though no information has been exchanged between the three scientists. This information is extremely difficult to conceptualize, because there is nothing in our current understanding of time and space to explain how past events can be changed by present actions. Yet this is what happens in this experiment. It is not science fiction, and physicists are reliably duplicating these results.

Does this mean that you can literally change your past, through things you're doing right now? The jury is still out on that, but Lynne McTaggart has written about the many experiments scientists are conducting that show just such an effect on an everyday, "eyeball" level. There is a growing body of evidence and belief that changing the past is not only plausible, it may become a realistic possibility for us as we uncover the ramifications of quantum entanglement.

For now, whether or not you start experimenting with changing your past (read Lynne's work if you think I'm being silly - Lynne McTaggart, *The Intention Experiment*, New York: Free Press, 2008), you should definitely understand that the old separateness fish tank is passé. It can now be replaced with confidence by the entanglement paradigm.

You see, in the entanglement experiments I described, there is no identifiable reason that two objects should be communicating this way. We intuitively "know" they shouldn't be. They can be separated by incredibly vast space and still exchange information instantaneously, which should not be possible since they are not in physical contact and the exchange is happening faster than the speed of light. The two entangled particles remain connected as if they are in direct contact with each other.

Additionally, the famous quantum, double-slit experiment (which you read about in the previous chapter) tells us it is **your** expectations that command subatomic particles to manifest into concrete objects. In this way, quantum physics shows us that entanglement runs even deeper—to the very core of all of our physical experiences. You are not only connected in a very real way to other objects, but your physical experiences are the direct result of a union (or co-mingling) between "you" and the quantum field. "You" are never a separate, distinct, neutral observer of your life experiences. You'll notice that I put "you" in quotes, because entanglement basically tells us that there is not an actual "you" in the way you've always thought.

The entanglement paradigm allows you to have a much better fish tank when trying to achieve your goals because it frees you from thinking of yourself as a detached observer without influence in the experiences unfolding in front of you. This doesn't mean that your actions will never have the desired effect, nor does it mean there is no value in following good directions to achieve your desired outcomes; it simply means, since your energy is co-mingling with the energy of all you are observing, you can now consider your expectations to be just as important as your actions. Your preconceptions have just as much impact on any experience as the specific actions you're taking.

Chapter Eight: The New Fish Tank of Nonlinearity

"In classical physics, the past is assumed to exist as a definite series of events, but according to quantum physics, the past, like the future, is indefinite and exists only as a spectrum of possibilities. Even the universe as a whole has no single past or history."

Stephen Hawking
Physicist
Nobel Prize Winner

The final new paradigm from quantum physics is nonlinearity. Classical physics had taught the world that systems are linear and created the paradigm of logical outcomes. In other words, you could expect logical outcomes to rule the effects of actions you take, as well as the responses and functioning of systems. The effects, when using the old fish tank of logical outcomes, should always be proportional to the action taken. This fish tank, like the others from the first scientific revolution, has had a deep and pervasive impact on the modern Western world.

To illustrate this old paradigm of logical outcomes, think of those sledgehammer games you find at carnivals. You hit a lever with a mallet or sledgehammer and force a weight into the air, with the goal of forcing the weight high enough to ring a bell. Ring a bell and, of course, you win a prize. When you play this game, you expect that the more force you bring to bear on the lever, the higher the weight will soar in proportion to the impact. The logical outcome paradigm of the first scientific revolution works the same way.

The Greek philosopher Aristotle is credited with creating the foundation of our familiar, classical logic. Prior to Aristotle, people believed that anything in the past that is true also has to be true today. Aristotle introduced the Western world to the idea that things are neither true nor false until they can be verified by their actual occurrence. The idea that we have to wait until something happens before we can verify it as true or false is the groundwork for the modern paradigm of logical outcomes, which states that things can be either "A" or "B," but not "A" *and* "B" at the same time. The first scientific revolution verified this concept, and it was then spread throughout Western society in the same manner as the other three paradigms.

Quantum physics, however, tells us the opposite – that all possibilities are present and inherent right now, in this moment. The plethora of possibilities actually all exist simultaneously in this present moment; things are not just "A" or "B," but also "C" through "Z." And the nonlinearity paradigm teaches us that we now no longer need to wait for a contingency to materialize as a time-space event to fully embrace all these possibilities in this moment. The nonlinearity fish tank shows us that, while we will eventually experience a definitive, concrete time-space event (or outcome), we can influence that outcome to a much greater degree than we ever thought possible using the old, logical, fish tank. This is possible precisely because of the literal existence of infinite possibilities, each as real as any other, which are always present in each moment. In fact, quantum theory actually considers that all the other possible outcomes that you did not cause to collapse from the quantum possibility wave may exist in parallel universes right now.

Like the others, the old-science fish tank of logical outcomes makes sense to you because you were raised to believe it. The logical outcome paradigm is so ingrained in our modern society that it would be impossible to chronicle all the instances of it. So let's simply examine one area where we can find it: in the securing of a primary romantic relationship such as a marriage or union between two people. You undoubtedly share the common human desire for a loving commitment from an invested partner who not only supports you but also accepts you for who you are. Conversely, you also probably want to return these wonderful gifts to your partner.

So the logical outcome paradigm dictates that you put a tremendous amount of effort and energy into your partner and your partnership, since it is so important. During your search for your partner, for example, you exert great effort into both your search for such a person and also your personal presentation to attract a desirable mate to you. And, when you begin spending time with a good partnership candidate, you put even more energy into the relationship as the courtship progresses.

When a long-term relationship does finally materialize for you, you work diligently to maintain your status as a continually desirable mate so your partner will be happy. Simultaneously, you attend to your partner's desires in the relationship to ensure his/her satisfaction with you. These actions taken to ensure a satisfying partnership follow the old logical outcome paradigm. You're not only striking the relationship "lever" with all the force you can muster, but you also expect that the relationship "bell" will ring loudly because of your efforts.

Yet one needs only a cursory read of data from Americans for Divorce Reform to understand the limitations of this old paradigm regarding relationships. Marital dissatisfaction remains very high. As many as half of all marriages end in divorce. Infidelity is even openly advocated on dating websites that advertise nationally. Almost half of all married Americans find their dreamed-of partnership ending much earlier than they planned.

This particular example may not be relevant to you because you may have a wonderful partnership. And, if this is the case, I don't want to alarm you because it's quite possible you have been unconsciously adhering to many (or all) of the principles found in the new paradigm of nonlinearity. But even if you are currently enjoying a satisfying romantic relationship, I doubt you'd pass up an opportunity to find a better fish tank that will allow you to enjoy even more freedom in this area. Additionally, even if you're enjoying a wonderful partnership, I also imagine it's not difficult for you to see that the limitations of this old paradigm are causing a lot of people to suffer the heartbreak of unrealized dreams.

You may be tempted to place the blame for American's high divorce rate on our not being able to fulfill our commitments or on our poor choices when choosing a mate. I will counter that no one enters into a romantic relationship without the desire to make it a fulfilling one. Additionally, that desire is going to lead most people to put every ounce of their abilities into making that relationship successful. After all, what other fish tank has been available to guide us anyway? I hope you can dismiss the notion that our current divorce rate can be blamed simply on a proliferation of naïve hopes or an unwillingness to put forth the effort for relationships to succeed.

So, if the fault lies neither with a lack of desire nor an unwillingness to put forth the necessary efforts, what is the solution? After all, being involved in a committed and caring relationship is not only one of our most common desires, it is also a basic human need. And how hard is it, really, to work together with a mate, taking steps to ensure that the two of you will communicate, cooperate, and stay together through good times and bad?

The fault lies in a reliance on the old logical-outcomes paradigm. And the pain comes from not embracing the infinite multitude of possibilities that exist in this moment and from a dogged (yet inaccurate) belief that our outcomes will follow a logical sequence arising from the events preceding them. Once again, I recall little Splash's discouraging results and propose that it's time to get a better fish tank. This fish tank will be one where the simple actions of maintaining a relationship that you desire can make it work the way you believe it ought to. And, once again, this better fish tank from quantum physics will have power to help you achieve any goal, not just a loving, romantic relationship.

Quantum physics has forced us to rethink everything we thought we knew about logical outcomes. No longer should we think of formative events (or things that cause outcomes) as sequences that bring a predictable result for us. That is the paradigm of classical physics. The nonlinearity paradigm allows us to think of formative events as simply leading to potential outcomes or results.

The reformation of the logical outcomes paradigm of the first scientific revolution, which quantum physics has forced us to do, has led to the creation of a new fish tank: nonlinearity. In the nonlinearity paradigm measurement can actually be regarded as a somewhat primitive concept. And quantum physics is far from settled on this matter; theorists are still working to reconcile the open-endedness of quantum physics with its non-classical structure. Suffice it to say, due to quantum physics' indeterminate nature and its complex correlation, the old axiom that things can be "A" or "B" but not "A" *and* "B" no longer can be applied with assurance. This is true on every level of quantum theory.

As you have learned, quantum physics describes a relatively unpredictable universe where nothing is created except in context to an observer and her expectations. Since each observer is incredibly unique in her personal expectations, physicists have remarked that each observer will see her own universe. Within such a paradigm, it is extremely difficult (if not impossible) to use the old paradigm of logical outcomes. And it is equally impossible to experience anything but continual frustration if we cling to the logical-outcomes fish tank.

The nonlinearity paradigm does not tell us that we can no longer expect desirable outcomes when we take action or do footwork to achieve a goal. But it does free us from unrealistic expectations of those results and, freed from those expectations, we can begin to open ourselves up to new possibilities. Think of the nonlinearity paradigm as one where you take the handcuffs off our universe. You no longer have to paint the universe into a corner by demanding, through your specific and limited perspective of what constitutes a successful outcome, that your results must conform to a certain format for you to be happy. You can learn to be more readily open to the unexpected, which is a great tool considering you are certain to find plenty of that in your life.

Chapter Nine: The New, Unified Fish Tank of Architecture

"Quantum theory thus reveals a basic oneness of the universe. It shows that we cannot decompose the world into independently existing smallest units. As we penetrate into matter, nature does not show us any isolated 'building blocks', but rather appears as a complicated web of relations between the various parts of the whole. These relations always include the observer in an essential way. The human observer constitutes the final link in the chain of observational processes, and the properties of any atomic object can be understood only in terms of the object's interaction with the observer."

Fritjof Capra
Physicist

Now you have four new fish tanks from the super accurate science of quantum physics. And, while I hope you are excited to learn about these changes, it might also be a little overwhelming to determine how you can best utilize this new information in your life right now. To that end, I give you a unified paradigm that combines all four into a single new fish tank. After explaining this unified paradigm, I will spend the rest of this book giving you instructions for how you can employ it on a "street-level" basis - because, after all, that's the real reason to learn about quantum physics. What's additionally exciting to me, however, is that by practicing this new paradigm I'm certain you will discover other ramifications of it in your life and additional ways to use it. Because, as an active practitioner of this paradigm, I fully expect that you can help me use it even more completely if you're willing to share your experiences with me.

The unified paradigm found by combining the four new fish tanks about which you've just read is called architecture. It is so named because, by using it, you will truly become, with practice, the architect of your universe. My experience is that the architecture paradigm represents a next evolutionary step for human beings, and I am excited to introduce it to you. Having used this fish tank myself for many years, I look forward to seeing where this powerful paradigm takes you and I hope you share your journey with me as you employ it in your own unique ways and allow me to add your own experiences to mine.

The fish tank of architecture can be studied and employed in the same manner that the law of attraction currently is by millions of people. Quantum physics doesn't attempt to prove the law of attraction, but this paradigm does give scientific validation to the concept as I have come to understand it. I am not sure whether quantum physics is explaining the law of attraction or whether the law of attraction is explaining quantum physics - and I'm not sure it even matters. But law of attraction enthusiasts will find their beliefs and practices endorsed and enhanced by this paradigm.

Of seminal importance for this unified paradigm is an understanding that nothing in the material universe is a preexisting entity. No material object exists independent of you, awaiting your discovery. You are, literally, the creator of all that you see. Remember the old philosophical question "If a tree falls in the forest and no one is there, does it make a sound?" It turns out that if there is no one there, there is no forest at all. The material world is actually a comingling of your nonphysical energy with the energy of the quantum field, which is an unbounded, unformed field of energy representing the possibility to become anything.

In the architecture paradigm, we learn that the creation of the material world is not a bottom-up process as classical physics and your naked eye led you to believe. Instead, the creation of the material world is a top-down process. You already know that it is your observations and, more precisely, your expectations that command the unformed quantum field to manifest into concrete, distinct material objects. Physicists call this process "collapsing the quantum possibility wave," because all subatomic particles exist in a state of mere potential until our attention is placed upon them. You collapse the quantum possibility wave any time you awaken your senses and observe, which is an act that commands subatomic particles to abandon their state of potential and respond to your expectations to form material objects. This process is exactly why we can call this process a comingling of our energy with the universe. Material objects are created solely in context with you, the observer.

For the purposes of your new architecture paradigm, let's next look at where your expectations come from. Your expectations are derived almost wholly from your beliefs; what you believe dictates what you expect. For example, if you believe that you are a worthwhile, competent person who receives good things in some aspect of her life, you will expect those good things in that aspect of your life; thus, those expectations will command the quantum field to deliver them. Unfortunately, as you're all too aware, the quantum field does not care whether your beliefs align with your heart's desires and delivers unwanted manifestations just as reliably as desired ones (I'll explain this, and how to rectify the problem, in greater detail later). The quantum field doesn't care if a physical manifestation is experienced as good or bad, only that it matches up with your expectations.

The next logical question for exploring the architecture paradigm is this: Where do your beliefs come from? While a belief carries with it the overwhelming feeling of being "correct," you must understand that any belief you hold is correct only for you. A belief is not independently correct, nor should it be assumed to universally apply to everyone (or anyone) else. Why not? Because a belief is nothing more than something you have told yourself for so long that it has assumed that mantle for you and you alone. (I'll go into greater detail about this later).

In this manner, everything you see when you are observing the world with your senses is but a mirrored reflection of your energy. Your expectations are the commands that are channeling your internal energy. In fact, the sensation that you are a completely separate entity from every other physical manifestation of this universe is but an overwhelmingly strong illusion that can be explained through quantum physics. Each observer, physicists explain, sees her own individual universe—and this is meant to be taken literally, not metaphorically. You see, physicists call a material object in the universe a "time-space event." A time-space event is a group of subatomic particles, a part of the quantum field, that have abandoned their status as mere potential because they have been observed and commanded to assume a concrete, definitive form. Your body, your chair, your home, your neighbor, your car, and any other material object are all examples of subatomic particles that have been commanded, through your observations and expectations, to form into a time-space event. Material reality is simply the subatomic particles' temporary deviation from their previously unformed state.

The common experiences of physical life in our universe that most of us in the Western world share can be thought of as communal, unconscious agreements we all hold. Trees have green foliage, people age and grow old, water is liquid and flows downhill – these are examples of the agreements we've all unconsciously adopted about our material world. These agreements also apply to our more esoteric manifestations of life on Earth, such as wealth being conferred to those who work hard or have special skills and good deeds being valued by society. This helps to explain why, although we are creating our individual universes, we share so many common experiences regarding the physical world's manifestation.

But another key to the unified fish tank of architecture is to understand that "you" are actually not a time-space event. I should warn you: That was a trick statement. After all, in the previous paragraph, I wrote that your body is a time-space event. But the truth is, your body is not "you." It is not who you really are. The real "you" is a nonphysical energy that is currently using your body to have physical experiences.

And not only is your body not the real "you," neither is your brain. Your brain is merely an elegant tool for your nonphysical energy to use, just like your heart, lungs, skeleton, etc. But since your brain has some unique functionality to dialogue with you in spoken word, it is very important to understand just how easily it dupes you into accepting it as the real "you." Your brain has, in fact, undoubtedly co-opted your identity and fooled you into accepting it as who you are. But, like the Norse God Loki, your brain is a trickster.

Do not be angry with your brain for fooling you. It desperately wants to be who you are and is afraid of not being who you are because it understands that its existence is finite. Your brain, or your ego (as psychologists refer to it), can only retain its identity as "you" if you remain consciously unaware of your true self—the nonphysical energy that is really who you are.

Another powerful ally your brain has on its side is that the material reality you create is not a function of free will and creativity. The material reality you create is actually formed, 99.9% of the time, by the habitual firing of energy through your brain's preestablished neural network. In other words, you command the quantum field to form that which you already know, those things about which you have preestablished, habitual patterns of thought. This is a convenient and handy physical adaptation of the human brain that saves you from having to completely form your world anew with each observation of the quantum field (which is what a baby, who has yet to form an adult's neural pathways of habitual thought, does). This handy tool, our brain's neural pathways of habitual thought, is actually designed to shortcut the process of constant seminal creation and allows you to live a normal, adult life on our planet. And because your brain is the repository of these neural networks, it is easy to believe the façade that your brain (and, thus, "you") are experiencing free will and choice in your life.

But, as much as you rely upon your preestablished, habitual patterns of thought to continually re-create your material reality, there still exists a measurable fraction of a second between the time you observe the quantum field and the time your preestablished neural networks of habitual thought kick in. This millisecond is called the precognitive moment and has been referenced by psychologists since the late 1960s. This precognitive moment is where all creativity and freedom are found, since it exists prior to your brain's "auto-complete" functions kicking in. And it is in this moment that quantum consciousness researchers believe we have access to our nonphysical energy (the real "you"). When in conscious contact with the real you, and by expanding that moment intentionally through practiced focus, we open ourselves up to the limitless possibilities that the quantum field actually offers us.

Just how creative and free can you become? While I have not found it possible to alter the physical laws that govern our material existence on Earth (for example, I cannot fly or breath water), it is well documented that some people can alter them. For example, it has been long known that yogis and mystics (as practitioners of Eastern philosophy are often called) can, by entering deep meditative states, slow their breathing and heart rate so much that they can remain buried underground for long periods of time and survive (where you or I would suffocate). Perhaps practiced access to the precognitive moment (whether done intentionally or unconsciously) explains other rare human phenomena like precognition or remote viewing, which are skills our government has actually contracted gifted people to employ for national security purposes.

What can you expect when you also begin to intentionally access the precognitive moment, as you fully employ the unified paradigm of architecture? While you may never glimpse into the future or levitate (those aren't any of my goals, but please contact me immediately if you do anything like that.), I can guarantee you a few things. You will become a more conscious, more intentional creator of the time-space events that make up your life and, in doing so, you will become a happier, more successful person who comes much closer to aligning your dreams and goals with your physical experiences. You will see a different universe as you grow in awareness and ability because you will become a different "you."

In other words, within the architecture paradigm, as your beliefs change, so will your expectations, and so will your physical world. And, just as your beliefs and expectations are unique and different from mine, so too will you see and experience a different world than me. How different? That merely depends on how different our beliefs and expectations happen to be.

Another huge benefit you'll receive from what you're about to learn is that you will greatly expand your access to the precognitive moment. The three steps I'll teach you in the next chapter, combined with the six steps you'll discover in Chapter 11, will all increase that moment for you and that moment is where you have free interplay with the unlimited creativity and abundance of the quantum field. Having a practiced and extended audience with the precognitive moment, I've found, is a certain way to open yourself up to far greater possibilities than you've been accustomed to. Your experiences will no longer hold the same meanings for you because you will no longer be as locked in to your neural network of habitual thought as you create your reality on a daily basis.

One other thing about the real you that is important for you to know in regards to the architecture fish tank you're now going to inhabit: Since energy cannot be destroyed and since the real you is most definitely a nonphysical energy, it is only reasonable to accept that the real you can also never be destroyed. You cannot cease to exist and, by extension, you must have always existed. The real you is actually part of the larger quantum field and must be eternal. Does this fact speak to aspects of religious faith such as having a soul, the existence of a Holy Spirit, and eternal life? I'll leave that for you to decide.

Chapter Ten: How to Use the Fish Tank of Architecture on a Daily Basis to Achieve Your Dreams and Goals

"There literally are different worlds in which we live. The macroscopic world that we see is the world of ourselves, is the world of our atoms, the world of our nuclei. These are each totally different worlds. They have their own language, they have their own mathematics. They're not just smaller. Each is totally different, but they're complimentary because I am my atoms, but I am also myself. I am also my macroscopic physiology. It's all true. They're just different levels of truth. The deepest level of truth covered by science and by philosophy is the fundamental truth of unity. At that deepest sub-level of our reality you and I are literally one."

John Hagelin
Physicist

Neurologists and neuropsychologists tell us that traumatic events and near-death experiences can have the amazing effect of, essentially, wiping clean the brain's neural pathways of habitual thought. Someone who has died and been brought back or someone who has suffered deep emotional trauma (such as the death of an intimate loved one, bankruptcy, divorce, or estrangement from family) has actually been given a gift – that is, a fresh start, a clean slate, where she can create neural pathways of her choosing to replace her old, practiced habits of thought.

The reason such a clean slate can be called a gift relates to how our neural pathways of habitual thought, which become our beliefs, are formed. For 99% of us, our beliefs are given to us, or transferred to us, mostly during our childhood, from parents, teachers, and the popular culture. I don't believe that anyone has intentionally bestowed self-limiting beliefs upon you, but I am certain about three things:

1. Humans are inherently flawed and scarred creatures. Adults try to protect children and keep them from being hurt, so they pass along what they have been taught. But sometimes, either consciously or unconsciously, they pass along some rather limiting beliefs to their children. I know I've done it inadvertently with my own children. For example, I used to focus almost entirely on guiding and directing my childrens' actions, rather than emphasizing the importance of how they feel about any action they take.

2. The primary goal of popular culture is to sell something. Most dangerous is the predominant aspect of our popular culture that is selling not a hard good, but a belief system—such as the need to constantly consume or the need to fit in and be "cool" (through buying their products, of course). Since popular culture's primary aim is to sell, it is ultimately unrealistic to expect it to be concerned with instilling uplifting beliefs to us, unless those beliefs coincidentally happen to further its aim.

3. Even self-actualized people who are truly interested in your person growth and success are still limited by what they actually know. And, until only recently, everyone "knew" that the old fish tanks from the first scientific revolution were the "truth" and the best belief system we had. Hence that is what they passed on to you.

This chapter is special. It will teach you how to use the architecture fish tank. You will learn, in three steps, how to reform your neural patterns of habitual thought and utilize the architecture paradigm on a "street-level" basis to change your day-to-day life and see a new universe. If you have suffered a traumatic event recently, these instructions will be an easy blueprint for creating a beautiful new neural net of thoughts that produce beliefs that serve and uplift you. But if you haven't recently suffered a traumatic event (and I certainly hope that is the case for you), such an event will now not be a necessary ingredient to form a fantastically effective new neural platform of habitual thought. Each day, dutifully adhere to the steps that follow and, over the course of time (how long will vary for each individual), you will create an entirely new set of better beliefs. And, since your beliefs consciously and unconsciously drive your expectations, you will see a new and better universe—one much more closely aligned with your unique dreams and desires.

Step One - Understanding Storytelling

"The layman always means, when he says 'reality' that he is speaking of something self-evidently known; whereas to me it seems the most important and exceedingly difficult task of our time is to work on the construction of a new idea of reality."

Wolfgang Pauli
Physicist
Nobel Prize Winner

To begin making the full and best use of the new unified architecture paradigm, you need to develop a new habit that sounds very simple yet is based on the way you create your beliefs and, in turn, your expectations. And this new habit will allow you to reform your neural network of habitual thought to create new beliefs that serve you and bring you more into alignment with your dreams and goals. This new habit is probably the single most important component to implementing and using all the wonderful new tools you'll learn about in the rest of this book. It will be the foundation of your new life.

Your new habit is this: You're going to stop "telling it like it is" and start "telling it how you want it to be." You'll soon see that the habit you currently have of "telling it like it is" is actually a bad one because all it does is reinforce your existing neural network of habitual thought. In other words, it validates all of your old, limiting fish tanks.

To stop "telling it like it is" and start "telling it how you want it to be," you will begin with a vital premise that will have great power for the creation of your new life and the implementation of your new fish tanks. It's vital that you understand and embrace the following idea: No event or circumstance is inherently "good" or inherently "bad." No event or circumstance awaits you in a preexisting state of "goodness" or "badness." There is no such thing.

Please read the following very carefully: What makes something good or bad is not the thing itself but the story you choose to tell yourself about it. The term "story" in this context simply refers to the subjective and personal meaning and value you assign to each thing, event, and circumstance in your life. And you tell yourself that story via your constant inner dialogue.

Here is an example that illustrates how your story makes something good or bad for you. You and a friend sit on a park bench and watch people walking their dogs on a beautiful spring day. A man strolls by, being pulled along by a frisky black Labrador retriever. You are immediately captivated by this person's physical attractiveness and alluring aura, and you tell your friend so. Your friend, however, says that she hardly noticed the dog-walker and found that person rather plain and not attractive at all.

You both saw the same exact person yet had two completely divergent experiences. You found this person "good" (or in this case "attractive"), while your friend experienced this person as "bad" (or "not attractive"). Obviously, this dog-walker did not wait for your observations in a predetermined state of "good" or "bad." It was your unique story, the value you assigned him, that created an "attractive" or "unattractive" dog walker. And, yes, that story, or value, you assigned was based on a plethora of criteria that are personal and unique to you. The dog-walker was "desirable" not independent of you but entirely in context with you. Your personal preferences, which led to the story of "desirable" you told, are an example of your practiced neural patterns of habitual thought. Your experience of seeing an "attractive" man was not based on the man being independently "attractive" (because, after all, your friend saw him as "unattractive"). He was attractive because you told a story about him based on your patterns of habitual thought.

To lay the foundation for using the architecture paradigm, it is vital for you to understand how this works—that whether something is "good" or "bad" is the result of you comingling with that person, place, or thing via the story you are telling about it. You do this with every single event or circumstance in your life. Every moment of your life, you tell a story about every single person, place, event, and circumstance, proclaiming every aspect of your life experience either "good" or "bad" (or "wanted" or "unwanted"). Up to this point, by the way, I've placed quotes around these value terms to illustrate how subjective and personal they are. I'm going to mostly stop using quotes now, because I'll assume you've gotten the point. So when I write "good" or "bad," you'll now know that the my use of the word refers to the unique, subjective story you're telling.

There is nothing wrong with you doing this. Telling a story about everything (personally assigning value to everything) seems to be an integral part of the human experience. Your goal is not to stop telling these stories right now. You may do that later, after you've had more practice with the architecture fish tank, but all you need to do now is fully understand that you do tell these stories and that it's your story that makes something good or bad for you.

Here's an illustration:

An old farmer had only one horse, and one day it ran away. When the neighbors came to console the farmer over his terrible loss, the farmer said, "What makes you think it is so terrible?"

A month later, the horse came home, bringing with her two beautiful wild horses. The neighbors became excited at the farmer's good fortune. "Congratulations!" they proclaimed. "Such lovely, strong horses!" The farmer said, "What makes you think this is good fortune?"

While training the wild horses, the farmer's son was thrown from one of them and broke his leg. All the neighbors were very distressed. "Such bad luck! We are so sorry for your misfortune," the neighbors wailed. The farmer said, "What makes you think it is bad?"

A war came. Every able-bodied young man in the community was conscripted and sent into battle, where they ultimately died. Only the old farmer's son, because he had a broken leg, remained behind and lived.

No one would have blamed the farmer had he ascribed each event as good or bad (as the neighbors had done). After all, it seems that any rational person would see the goodness or badness of each turn of that tale. Yet, as this tale so beautifully illustrates, each event was eventually revealed to be the exact opposite of our expectations of what would be good or bad. The initial story the farmer might have told himself about each event, although logical and reasonable, would have been proven wrong in the long run.

The old farmer's resolve to not tell a story about each event, defining its value, isn't supposed to make us feel like unenlightened simpletons because we choose to make such judgments about everything we encounter. The main point of this tale is to remind us that those stories are only our subjective judgments, not the unchangeable and unyielding label of "truth" we almost always bestow upon them. And, furthermore, the tale teaches us that our judgments are optional. Whatever story you decide to tell is purely your choice.

Here are some examples of common life events and the rational stories you might tell about them:

1. Getting an email from your friend is good, because it means she cares about you and likes you.

2. Getting your gas and electric bill is bad, because the rates are too high and your already limited bank account is being squeezed.

3. Getting positive results from your latest medical exam is good, because it means you're healthy.

4. Your daughter's poor grades on her report card are bad, since it means she is a currently failing in school.

And most anyone would agree with such good or bad values if you placed them on each event, because they're reasonable and sensible interpretations of the events described.

Yet, like the tale of the old farmer, any of these stories might be shown to be inaccurate interpretations. Perhaps the good checkup from your doctor fills you with some false confidence and you slack off on healthy habits—which might make that positive medical report actually a bad thing, right? Perhaps your daughter's poor grades are the final straw that motivates her to get her act together and reach her academic potential. Then those horrible grades weren't actually bad, correct? Or are they? Just like the farmer's tale, we could go on and on with these illustrations of how subjective our stories of good and bad can be.

The point is not that we should stop telling stories about life's events and circumstances. We will continue to do that. We're such good storytellers that we put Mother Goose to shame. The point is for you to realize that your stories of good and bad are not "telling it like it is" as you've always assumed; your stories are "telling it the way you're choosing to tell it"! The stories you tell yourself are entirely subjective and entirely your choice. And, as you're about to find out, embracing this premise will make all the difference in your success in achieving your dreams and goals.

Obviously, you are reading this book because you desire more success in your life. You want to more completely achieve your unfulfilled aspirations. And your frustration with having unfulfilled aspirations is a direct by-product of a specific problem you have developed with your storytelling that, when solved, will allow you to freely use your new, unified architecture fish tank and, in relatively short order, become much more closely aligned with your unique dreams and goals. Conversely, until you solve your storytelling problem, all the self-help instructions in the world won't get you any closer. Allow me to illustrate your storytelling problem through three examples. You may find these examples odd or even unsettling, but read through them carefully because they illustrate what you must change.

Let's start with an example of a make-believe event with a very obvious story you'd tell about it: kicking an innocent puppy out a tenth-story window. If you surveyed everyone in your city, every person would definitely say that kicking a puppy out a window is bad. I concur and I'm sure you do too. But that does not mean that the act of kicking a puppy out a window is inherently bad; it means we are all telling the same story about it. We all make the same judgment—and rightfully so. I wouldn't expect anyone to say, "I'm not going to call kicking a puppy out the window 'bad' because that's merely a story I'm telling myself; kicking a puppy out the window might be good." Kicking a puppy out a window is bad.

And here's the most important point of this first example. Because you, like everyone else, tell yourself that kicking an innocent puppy out a tenth-story window is bad, I know you would never kick a puppy out a tenth-story window.

For our second example, let's use an unsettling event with a less obvious story you'd tell about it: forcing someone to leave a homeless shelter where he has been staying. If you surveyed everyone in your city, you would undoubtedly get a mixed reaction of good and bad. Some stories would angrily call the action bad, as in "You're taking away his last hope and all but signing his death certificate." While other stories might call the action decidedly good, as in "You're making room for someone more deserving and this is probably the tough love he really needs to get motivated to change his life." We'd probably find most of the stories falling somewhere in between those two extremes.

Which story is the "truth"? Is it good or is it bad to force a person out of a homeless shelter where he has been staying? You already know that the correct answer to that question is that the "truth" is subjective. Whether it is good or bad is all based upon whatever story you tell yourself. But, unlike the first example, can't you easily see that even though someone else's story might be different from yours, there is still understandable logic and reason behind their story?

This once again illustrates just how subjective, unique, and individual your story is regarding whether a person, place, thing, event, or circumstance is good or bad.

And here's the most important point of this second example: Whether or not you would force a person to leave a homeless shelter would depend on the story you told yourself about that action. And, while I don't know you personally, I'll bet I know this about you: You wouldn't force a homeless person to leave a shelter if the story you told about that action made it bad. And, alternatively, you would only force him to leave if the story you told about that action made it good.

Finally let's use an example of a seemingly innocent action: eating a big, gooey, decadent, hot, fresh cinnamon roll for breakfast. What story would the people of your city tell about that action? You'd get a really mixed bag, to be sure, without nearly as many strong-feeling stories as in the first two examples. What would your story be? Is it good or is it bad to eat a delicious cinnamon roll for breakfast?

You might be surprised to learn that the important point of this example is not whether you think it's good or bad to eat a big, gooey, decadent, hot, fresh cinnamon roll for breakfast. The most important point about this example is: When you tell yourself that eating a cinnamon roll is bad and you eat it anyway, you have just guaranteed that your dreams and goals (if they relate to weight loss) are going to remain out of your reach. This, in a nutshell, is the storytelling problem that's played such a pivotal role in keeping your life's success farther away from you than you'd like.

So let's recap these three examples. You would never kick a puppy out of a tenth story window because that is bad. And you would never force a person out of a homeless shelter if you called that action bad. But, on a daily basis, you may be eating food (or doing something else that is not furthering your goals) that you're telling yourself is bad and somehow thinking you can escape the consequences. And, in relation to the achievement of your goals and dreams, the opposite is also true. Not doing something you call good is just as much a part of the storytelling problem you need to solve.

Doing something you call bad and expecting desired results violates your new architecture paradigm, just as **not** doing something you call good and expecting desired results does. Telling yourself that something is bad and doing it anyway, or telling yourself something is good and not doing it, are huge problems and are, in fact, your storytelling problem. This storytelling problem is the main reason you have been separated from your dreams and goals.

The words you're using to tell stories about yourself are as important as the stories themselves. In fact, you should never again refer to yourself using ugly words like "failure," "dumb," "can't," etc. When you use such ugly words in your stories about yourself, you almost always *feel* ugly too. In fact, try an ugly-word experiment right now regarding the goal of weight loss (whether you desire to lose weight or not). Say out loud, "I am fat." How did that feel? Now say out loud, "I have unwanted weight." If you're like me, saying "unwanted weight" felt a lot better than saying "fat."

Why are your words important? Because, just as the stories themselves are important, the words you use to tell your stories are meaningful and carry a punch. You'll learn even more about their importance later. For now, here's why I never want you to refer to yourself using ugly words again. You are not your actions, nor are you the results of your actions. "Failure" (or any other ugly word) is not your state of being; "failure" does not define you as a human being and it is not what or who you are.

Go back to the two statements in our ugly-word experiment. Could you recognize the difference between "I am fat" and "I have unwanted weight"? I'll underline the words that make those two statements as different as night and day:

1. "I <u>am</u> fat."

2. "I <u>have</u> unwanted weight."

The first statement says that "fat" is who you are; the second statement says that you are merely experiencing unwanted weight but that the unwanted weight is not who you are. Just as I want you to start telling stories that serve you, I want you to use words that also serve you by uplifting and enhancing you, not degrading you. In this book, you're learning exactly how to do that.

It's time for you to start telling yourself new stories about every experience you have. And, in fact, you will find that your goals will be more fully realized only when you are telling these new stories, using better feeling words, and feeling better about yourself and your experiences right where you are. No longer do you have to repeat and believe those stories that hurt you and keep you imprisoned on the outside of your desires, looking with frustration at your unrealized aspirations.

Remember, your beliefs are not the "carved in stone" monuments of truth you've built them into. Your beliefs are merely the stories you've told yourself long enough that they have become your truths. That's right: Your beliefs are true for you simply because you've told yourself the stories so many times. And by telling yourself new stories, using new words, you will, slowly but surely, create new beliefs for yourself. Building new beliefs is like building a house; you do it one brick (or, in this case, one word and one story) at a time.

Solving this storytelling problem is the key to using the new architecture paradigm and to achieving your goals. So accepting that your stories define the value of all your experiences, learning to use better feeling words, and starting to tell better stories will allow you to employ the architecture fish tank.

Step Two - See Your Beliefs (and Your Feelings) Objectively

"Differences exist because thought develops like a stream that happens to go one way here and another way there. Once it develops it produces real physical results that people are looking at, but they don't see where these results are coming from — that's one of the basic features of fragmentation."

David Bohm
Physicist
Nobel Prize Winner

The next step you'll take to fully utilize your new architecture paradigm has already been alluded to in Step One. You are not your beliefs, nor are you even your feelings. Your beliefs and your feelings are incredibly important and you should never pretend they are anything different than what they currently are (that is usually called "being in denial" and it almost always leads to more pain and a continued spinning of your wheels, as far as reaching your dreams and goals are concerned). To the contrary, learning to view your beliefs and your feelings objectively will allow you to change them in ways that serve you mightily without denying their current status in your life.

Being in denial about your feelings and beliefs, pretending they're something other than what they really are, can actually get you in a lot of trouble with the architecture paradigm. Don't ever pretend you feel better than you really do or hold a more positive belief than you actually do. Positive affirmations and statements, positive intentions, and desires for positive outcomes do not always equate with your true beliefs. Later on, I'll examine this concept in greater detail with an example from my life, but for now understand that since the quantum field is responding to your true beliefs (and not your surface-level desires) when it manifests your physical reality, you can often fool yourself into thinking you have positive beliefs about something when you really don't. So it is very important to acknowledge your feelings and beliefs, just where they are currently, as you also learn not to personalize them. I'll talk about acknowledging your feelings and beliefs a bit more later, during Step Three, and in the last chapter I'll even teach you how you can find gratitude for them just as they are— even if they are far out of alignment with your dreams and goals.

Your beliefs, after all, are only your most practiced, habitual thoughts. Certainly your beliefs feel 100% true to you. After all, your beliefs were not only bestowed upon you by people and groups you trusted and/or allowed to influence you, but you are intimately familiar with them since you have held them and invested yourself in them for such a long time.

Your feelings, like your beliefs, are true for you (and you alone) and, because of that, shouldn't be discounted nor denied. Yet it's also very important to recognize that your feelings are simply emotional feedback for how closely your beliefs are currently aligning with your aspirations for yourself in this moment. While very real to you, they are not "facts."

As you practice objectifying your beliefs and feelings, by seeing them this way rather than personifying them as you have most likely spent your life doing, you will gain freedom from the power they currently have over your state of being. And you will gain the freedom to examine them without so much emotional investment. When you cut your finger, after all, you don't say, "I am now a sliced, physically imperfect human being." You simply say, "I currently have a cut on my finger (but my current state of having a cut is not who I am)."

Similarly, when you have a feeling, like sadness, you are not required to say, "I am sad" (as in the "I am fat" example from Step One). You can, instead, now say, "I am experiencing sadness in this moment (but sadness is not who I am)." That second statement still acknowledges your feeling—you're not in denial nor are you pretending you don't feel sad. However, the second statement makes it very clear that you are not your feelings; you are merely experiencing a feeling. And that distinction, as you've learned, makes a world of difference.

You can also start to do the same thing to depersonalize your beliefs (although your beliefs are not often as readily apparent and accessible to your conscious awareness as your feelings are). For example, instead of saying, "I have to find the perfect diet to finally be able to lose my unwanted weight, since the many I've used haven't worked" (which is a statement declaring your belief about how you will be able to lose weight), you can now say, "My current belief is that I have to find the perfect diet to be able to lose my unwanted weight." The second statement acknowledges your current belief without sugar-coating the truth; yet, by adding the prefix "My current belief is…," you depersonalize the belief and clearly identify that it is not who you are but merely your current, neural pathway of habitual thought that has been your truth for a while.

What these new ways of talking to yourself about your feelings and your beliefs will do is allow you to examine them objectively, without feeling as if you are held hostage by them. You can look at a feeling and ask yourself, "Why am I experiencing this unwanted feeling? What belief do I currently hold that is not allowing me to align myself (and my actions) with my desired outcome?" Additionally, you can look at a belief and ask yourself, "Why do I believe this, when it obviously doesn't align with my desired outcome? And what new stories can I begin to tell myself (and what new words should I be using), so that I can change this belief?"

I have explained, of course, that your beliefs create your expectations, and that your expectations create your physical experiences. Your beliefs are powerful and necessary things for the human experience. They are the internal "drivers" of your expectations that you will now learn to change and, when changed, will create a new universe for you to see. And your feelings are also powerful and necessary things for the human experience as well. They are tools that you can learn to use with great effectiveness.

Your feelings, once depersonalized, are amazing tools for you because they serve as the "thermometers" of your beliefs. Thermometers are pretty handy tools for knowing whether your body has a fever or not, aren't they. Your feelings are your built-in thermometers that tell you if your beliefs are currently serving your attainment of your dreams and desires, because they tell you if your beliefs are in congruence with your desires. What a great untapped asset!

In other words, your feelings tell you whether your current beliefs match up with your desired outcomes. If you feel good about something, that is the best sign that your current belief about it is a positive one and is aligned with your desired outcomes. And the opposite is also true. When you feel bad about something, you can be pretty sure you hold a current belief about it that is negative and/or not aligned with your desired outcomes. As you've learned, quantum physics teaches you that your beliefs create your expectations and your expectations create your reality. So paying attention to your feelings, yet taking away their power over your state of being by looking at them objectively, has amazing power. Your feelings are letting you know what your current beliefs are and therefore give you an opportunity to change those beliefs when you find they are not serving your realization of your goals.

Does the importance of paying attention to your feelings and beliefs mean that your actions are unimportant to the attainment of your goals? After all, the unity fish tank stresses the importance of your internal energy over the actions you take. Not at all. Your actions will always be important in the physical world. It's just that, contrary to what you've been taught, your actions are of secondary importance compared to how you feel about them (primarily because of what those feelings reveal about your beliefs).

Let me explain what I'm talking about and further illustrate how you can use the science of quantum physics in your everyday life. The entanglement paradigm suggests that when you focus on what you don't want or upon the absence of your desires, you not only feel bad, but you also get more of those very things you're focused on. This is because your physical experiences are entangled; you are not a separate entity from what you are observing. What you focus on is what grows. In other words, when you focus on the absence of a desired outcome or result, you will only find more of its absence. I know this can be a cruel irony, but people who chose to tell themselves better feeling stories about their current unwanted (but temporary) circumstances almost always find better experiences. But if you focus on the current absence of your desired circumstances (which, of course, feels bad), telling yourself some version of "This isn't the way it's supposed to be," you will usually only find more of their absence in your physical experiences.

I'm sure you've been taking a lot of good actions designed to achieve your unique dreams and goals, but you've continued to be frustrated by their absence because the stories you tell yourself are about your wanting them, needing them, and not having them. It ultimately comes down to this: When you constantly tell yourself some version of "It shouldn't be this way" or "Why don't I have this thing that I so desperately desire?" you're almost always going to feel bad and get more bad outcomes. Because your focus is on the absence of what you want, you've gotten the results the entanglement paradigm teaches you to expect: simply *more* of the absence of what you want.

Any failure, especially when you are making the unnecessary mistake of personalizing your beliefs and feelings, makes you feel even worse about yourself, prompting you to tell even more negative stories. Do you see the horrible, self-defeating, self-perpetuating pattern here?

But don't worry. I'm about to teach you how to retrain your thought process and grow new beliefs that will serve you. These new beliefs and the new expectations that will spring forth from them will help you achieve your dreams and goals a lot sooner than you ever thought possible.

Step Three - How to Tell New Stories

"If I am right in saying that thought is the ultimate origin or source, it follows that if we don't do anything about thought, we won't get anywhere. We may momentarily relieve the population problem, the ecological problem, and so on, but they will come back in another way."

David Bohm
Physicist
Nobel Prize Winner

To start telling new, better stories that will build new beliefs by creating new neural pathways of habitual thought, I hope you have embraced the idea that the type of story you tell about any event is completely your choice. I will certainly allow that some events and circumstances present more difficult challenges to tell a good story about, but that fact does not negate this idea. There is no rule that says you must tell any type of story about any event or circumstance.

A commitment to tell new, better stories takes a lot of willingness and some diligence, too. After all, you've had the bad habit of "telling it like it is" for your whole life until now. But who convinced you that any story has to be negative or bad? Is there a law that states that you are required to call a less-than-desirable experience bad? Nope, there is no such law. Calling any story bad is simply a choice you make (most likely unconsciously). And you can choose to do it differently, starting right now, if you truly want to create new neural pathways of habitual thought, form beliefs more in line with your desired outcomes, create new expectations that will arise from those new beliefs, and, thus, see and experience an improved universe. While this all may sound very simple, it is not necessarily easy to do. I will now teach you how to do it. And I assure you, it really works.

First, you must begin practicing using your feelings as thermometers as I described in Step Two. Any time you feel bad when experiencing any aspect of your physical reality, or even when thinking about your dreams and goals (or their absence), pay attention to that feedback. Your bad feelings are a redline signal that your beliefs on this subject, this aspect of your physical reality, are not in congruence with your desired outcomes for it. Don't disparage your bad feelings. They function just like pain from an injury to your body. They are alerting you to something that needs your attention so you can address it and change. In this case, they are alerting you to some beliefs you need to change if you want your desires to manifest in your physical reality. So embrace your feelings right where they are, since their feedback is your first-class ticket to knowing what beliefs you need to change.

When you do encounter a belief that is not aligned with your desired outcomes, do not begin to change your belief by telling outlandishly positive stories about it and your desired outcomes. This will not ring true for you and, thus, will not work to truly change your belief. Changing your beliefs, as I've written, is a process, and such an "overnight" change will not be believable to you. The best place to start the process of telling better stories is to begin exactly where you are.

One handy tool to self-diagnose exactly where you are regarding a belief is to inventory your true feelings about a desired outcome (or dream or goal). Take financial abundance, for example. Perhaps you're always dreamed of having more money, yet the real financial abundance you've desired has continually remained just out of your reach. You may have experienced things such as your car breaking down just as you were starting to get ahead in your checking account, and we all know how frustrating that can be. In this example, you should write the word "money" at the top of a blank sheet of paper and quietly listen to your gut-level, emotional response to the word. Although your top-of-mind awareness will undoubtedly scream, "I want more money!" if you really listen to your gut-level feelings you'll hear a different story. You'll hear messages like:
"I don't have enough."
"It never lasts when I get it."
"I'm underpaid."
"I'm not worthy of having a lot of it."
"It's greedy and bad to want more than I 'need.'"
"If I really had more than I do now, I'd be taking it away from someone else who needs it just as much as me."

These feelings represent your true current beliefs about money. There is nothing inherently wrong with having these beliefs, by the way, and you are under no obligation to change them. But these beliefs most definitely are not in alignment with your desire to have more money.

Perhaps you think it silly of me to claim that your true beliefs about money (or any other unrealized desire you have) are not your usual, top-of-mind feelings of "I want it." And any such reluctance to accept this premise is important to address. I can guarantee that, if you have an unrealized desire, dream, or goal, your true beliefs about that material object or experience are negative and not aligned with that desire. How can I make such a bold and seemingly presumptuous claim? Because of the new architecture paradigm that clearly teaches us exactly how our material reality is created. You are the creator of your material reality, as the quantum field responds perfectly to your beliefs and expectations when creating your material reality, so it is a certainty that your material experiences are a perfect match with your true beliefs. In other words, it is impossible to experience the absence of something desired if your beliefs about that desired thing are truly positive. So, if you are experiencing an absence of a desired outcome, your true, underlying beliefs about that thing must be negative. If they were truly positive, you would already be experiencing that desired outcome right now. This is exactly why it is so important to inventory your true beliefs about your absent desires in order to change them.

Although it may be tempting to view this aspect of the architecture paradigm in a negative light, I encourage you to see the freedom found through it. Am I saying that you are responsible for all your troubles, your suffering, and the absence of your desires? I suppose that's one way someone could choose to view it, but I choose to say that you are not responsible for your previous "failings" and, instead, are now responsible for your future "successes." I am not claiming that people in horrific circumstances, like abused children, are responsible for their circumstances. I have no explanation for abusive situations like this, nor do I intend to minimize them here. I do know, however, that for the attainment of the overwhelming majority of personal dreams and goals, even for people currently suffering greatly, there is tremendous freedom in the architecture paradigm, because, through it, you are no longer an unconscious victim of your old beliefs. The architecture paradigm does not teach you to blame yourself for your suffering. Instead, it teaches you to take responsibility for your freedom from suffering from this point forward.

Additionally, do not be surprised when you continue to experience unwanted results - even after practicing the architecture paradigm for years. And, most certainly, do not make the mistake of assuming you "wanted" those negative experiences or intentionally caused them. I'll explain later the important and necessary purpose of continued unwanted experiences and even reveal the secret of how and why you should feel profoundly grateful for them. There is truly no longer any impetus to blame yourself nor beat yourself up for negative or unwanted experiences.

There are many famous examples of people who overcame incredible suffering to survive against all odds by choosing to change their beliefs. One such person, Louis Zamperini, famously survived adrift on the Pacific Ocean without food or water for a record 47 days after his plane was shot down during World War II. Additionally, Zamperini survived an additional two-and-a-half years under brutal conditions in Japanese concentration camps. In her book, *Unbroken*, Laura Hillenbrand describes how Zamperini and a fellow pilot stayed alive by consciously deciding to tell stories of their choosing and change their beliefs to ones that served their survival. Zamperini spoke about consciously choosing to reframe his neural network of habitual thought when common sense told him that no one should survive on the ocean for as long as he did, nor under the inhuman and dehumanizing conditions of his subsequent imprisonment. Zamperini constantly told himself and his mates stories about what he would do with the remainder of his life, meals he would prepare, and how he would live. He even went so far as to devise an elaborate ritual of visualizing the preparation of sumptuous meals, literally pantomiming the food preparation, and describing the ingredients and the cooking processes in exacting detail.

Zamperini survived his ordeals—where most people under those circumstances did not—in large part because he refused to be limited by his old beliefs and by his commitment to creating new ones that served his desire to live. It bears mentioning that there were originally three survivors of that fateful plane crash. One of Zamperini's fellow survivors on their life raft refused to participate in his indomitable commitment to tell new stories and grow new beliefs, instead choosing to remain silent and withdrawn despite his mates' encouragement. That crew member slowly died at sea, withering away under the same horrifying circumstances that Zamperini and his fellow survivor overcame. Zamperini knew that he had a choice between telling bad stories and telling good stories and between believing he would die as most others would or believing he would live and, later, thrive. Regarding both of those choices, he chose the latter, and his chosen beliefs became, against all odds, his reality.

Viktor Frankl is another famous example of someone who took personal responsibility for overcoming unimaginable conditions of depravity and suffering by changing his beliefs. In his famous book, *Man's Search for Meaning*, Frankl describes his imprisonment in Auschwitz and four other Nazi concentration camps. Frankl watched his parents, brother, and pregnant wife die in these camps and came to understand that many of his fellow inmates were simply choosing to give in to their fate and resign themselves to death. He learned that he could choose how to cope with his suffering, chose to find and define meaning in it, and move forward with renewed purpose. By consciously choosing his beliefs, he described a freedom that eventually led him to actually feel pity for his Nazi oppressors because, even though he was the one behind the barbed wire, they were actually more imprisoned than he. They were held hostage by their stories and beliefs, where he was actually free because he had chosen to create his own uplifting, transcendent ones.

Frankl's book has given hope to millions. It is difficult to imagine how a person could rise above such circumstances and find personal growth amid them, let alone survive them in the first place. Yet Frankl did just that, through a commitment to define his reality by choosing beliefs that served his desire to live. His tale is a testament to the birthright we all share to tell stories and hold beliefs of our choosing, rather than succumb to conventional wisdom and accept what everyone would tell us is only common sense. I have, thankfully, never had to face such impossible odds and I hope you never have to, either. But, as these examples illustrate, we can be secure in the knowledge that the stories we tell and the beliefs we hold will always be our choice. The freedom we have to define our life in this manner gives hope to those of us whose suffering seems beyond inconsequential when weighed against what these men overcame.

Once you have spent enough quiet time to identify your true feelings and beliefs about an unrealized dream or goal, it is time for you to make a concerted effort to tell new, better stories about it. If you continually remind yourself to follow the directions from Step Two, to depersonalizing your feelings and beliefs, this process will be much easier for you because your emotional investment in those things will be lowered greatly. You won't view your feelings and beliefs as who you are but simply as feedback and temporary, current neural pathways of habitual thought, respectively.

Eventually you will be able to tell amazingly positive stories about your desires and almost any circumstance, but those types of stories won't be effective at first because you won't really believe them. Your beliefs and your desires are simply too far out of alignment currently for this kind of abrupt 180 degree change in your storytelling to be real for you. So the best method to use when you first start telling new, better stories, is to consciously insert the prefix "I currently believe (or feel)..." and the suffix "...but I believe that, with practiced effort, I can learn to tell better stories about (that thing or event) over the course of time." You might also add, "And if I consciously choose to tell better stories about (that thing or event), I believe that, over time, my beliefs will change about it and, thus, so will my material reality and experiences concerning it."

Let's revisit the tale of the man, his son, and the horses. Except this time I'll put the prefix and suffix I recommended into the two "bad" twists this tale takes to illustrate how you can use them.

An old farmer had only one horse, and one day it ran away. When the neighbors came to console the farmer over his terrible loss, the farmer said, "Although I currently believe this might be terrible, I also believe that, with practiced effort, I can learn to tell better stories about my horse running away, over the course of time. And if I consciously choose to tell better stories about my horse running away, I believe that, over time, my beliefs will change about it and, thus, so will my material reality and experiences concerning it. "

A month later, the horse came home, bringing with her two beautiful wild horses. The neighbors became excited at the farmer's good fortune. "Congratulations!" they proclaimed. "Such lovely, strong horses!" The farmer said, "What makes you think this is good fortune?"

While training the wild horses, the farmer's son was thrown from one of them and broke his leg. All the neighbors were very distressed. "Such bad luck! We are so sorry for your misfortune," the neighbors wailed. The farmer said, "Although I currently believe this might be bad, I also believe that, with practiced effort, I can learn to tell better stories about my son breaking his leg, over the course of time. And if I consciously choose to tell better stories about my son breaking his leg, I believe that, over time, my beliefs will change about it and, thus, so will my material reality and experiences concerning it. "

A war came. Every able-bodied young man in the community was conscripted and sent into battle, where they ultimately died. Only the old farmer's son, because he had a broken leg, remained behind and lived.

I suggest that you make it your private "job" to frame all of your belief (and feeling) statements this way. It will take some concerted effort on your part, to be sure, and you will undoubtedly forget often to do it at first. Don't be hard on yourself when you do forget, by the way. Remember that you're breaking a negative storytelling habit that you've cemented into your neural network through decades of practice. It will take time and patience for these new storytelling habits to become second nature, so don't be discouraged when you forget. Just gently stop your story and restate it using that prefix and suffix combination without beating yourself up.

It is not important to consciously remember all the bad stories you've told yourself and now "fix" them by retelling those stories using your new prefix and suffix. All you need to do is stay aware and listen to the stories you're currently telling, amending them immediately the moment you recognize that the stories are bad ones. You'll find that you've told yourself many of these bad stories for years and they will probably sound very familiar to you – they will sound like the truth, in fact. Don't worry about the bad stories you've told; focus on changing your stories from this point forward. Changing your neural pathways of habitual thought is done by changing your stories in the present moment, not by focusing on past behavior.

What you will find, with your continued practice, is that using the prefix and suffix combination as prescribed will open you up to seeing new possibilities. You will notice a new freedom to think about your life experiences in fresh, more positive ways and, thus, feel inspired to tell even better stories more readily. Use this freedom to experiment and play with the new, better stories you're telling about your life experiences. You may feel inspired to tell better stories about undesirable outcomes or circumstances such as "Perhaps this is happening just like it's supposed to, although I may lack the perspective to understand why right now" or "Maybe this experience is just what I need, although it might not seem to be from my current perspective" or "Although this is not what I desired, I can believe that this outcome is an improvement over my previous experiences, and I can believe that further improvements are possible if I keep practicing the three steps." Whether you tell yourself these stories or others unique to you, you will find that they become self-fulfilling prophecies, bringing incrementally better experiences into your material reality— just as the architecture fish tank tells you will happen.

Remember, too, that a large component of the new stories you're telling is the better words you're now using. Anytime you realize you're referring to yourself using ugly words like "stupid," "failure," or "I can't," stop and gently rephrase your statements using uplifting, or at least neutral, word choices. Don't berate yourself, either, when you catch yourself using ugly words. You've been using these words for a long time, and getting out of this habit is a process just like telling new stories. Instead of saying, "I can't buy this because, as usual, I don't have enough money," say, "I am choosing to not spend my money on this right now." Instead of saying, "I am a failure at money management; I'm always broke," say "I haven't had a lot of previous success with money management, but I'm open to learning how to do it better and I believe, with practice, I can do that." Your words, after all, carry a lot of emotional weight. Choose them wisely and your stories will automatically improve. They will start to guide your expectations toward better outcomes as they slowly reform your stories and change your beliefs.

Your goal is to finally be able to believe stories like "I expect success" and "I know I am successful at…." You'll get there eventually, with practice, if you stick to your commitment of telling better, believable stories. How long that will take depends on three variables:

1. How long you've held the limiting, negative beliefs that you're currently improving to align with your desires.

2. How greatly you desire to see an improved universe and realize your dreams and goals.

3. How diligently you focus on consistently telling yourself better stories and using uplifting words.

Another thing to consider regarding your decision and commitment to change your beliefs by telling better stories is this: You are going to be telling stories about every person, place, and thing you encounter every day for the rest of your life. Given this, doesn't it make sense to choose to tell better ones? Even if the changes don't happen overnight or as grandly as you might like at first, why would you choose not to tell better stories:

- Now that you have a choice between telling negative or positive stories

- Now that you understand how those stories have created (and continue to create) your neural pathways of habitual thought

- Now that you know your neural pathways of habitual thought become your beliefs

- Now that you know that your beliefs create your expectations

- Now that you know your expectations command the quantum field to form your physical reality

- Now that you know that changing your stories changes your beliefs

- Now that you know that changing your beliefs creates new expectations for you

- Now that you know that your new expectations will, literally, create a new universe for you to see

Since you're going to be telling stories all the time anyway, given all that you now know, why wouldn't you choose to tell better ones?

And, with practice, your new beliefs will not only grow, they will also become more and more solidified as your dominant neural pathways of habitual thought. Eventually, you won't merely be saying, "I am successful at (insert your goal)," and you won't even stop at believing it either. You will **be** that. And, at that stage, your dreams and goals will manifest into your physical experiences almost like magic because the quantum field of unformed subatomic particles will respond to your knowing in the way they always have. They will form a material reality for you that reflects your new expectations, which you have reformed to ensure their alignment with your dreams and goals. You don't even need to concern yourself with how all that will be accomplished because you can trust that not only will you have all the motivation and inspiration you'll need just when you need it, but so too will new, unexpected opportunities arise just when they are needed to ensure your success.

Understand that some people will scoff at these new paradigms and your plan to use them in your life. After all, they differ dramatically with everything most people "know" about life in our universe and can sound, to people not ready to hear them, like feel-good philosophies or even fairy tales. If you hear criticism, know that it's natural for our brains to be resistant to new ideas (especially when we are not willing to change and have minds that are still closed) almost as forcefully as our immune system resists a virus or pathogen. Since you are open to these new ideas, however, you are fortunate, and I'm sure you've already begun to feel and experience their truth and power. Your acceptance of these new fish tanks is validated by the fact that they're formed from an incredibly more accurate and precise body of science, quantum physics, than the old reasons you did things the ways you always did them.

I feel compassion towards such critics and I encourage you to do the same because, after all, they are merely having the same experiences that our little friend, Splash, did. They do not even realize that they, too, are adhering to old, ineffective paradigms that came from outdated science. Critics are often angered by someone who claims they can change their paradigms and see a new universe because they are still stuck in the unfortunate belief that this idea means they are personally to "blame" for their circumstances and are not yet open to the freedom these changes contain. In fact, most of these critics, like poor Splash, do not even realize they are in a fish tank at all.

People living in ill-suited fish tanks, you see, often get angry when they see another fish, like you, learn to swim in the open ocean while they still feel bitter about their current circumstances. My suggestion, should you encounter such criticism, is to concentrate on finding other, like-minded fish to hang with. You can love and feel compassion for these critics while serving as a living example, through your ever improving life, of how change is possible. And you can know that these critics will always be just as free to make the changes you've made. They, too, are just as capable of changing their fish tanks and being every bit as happy and free as you're becoming.

Before we end this chapter about the three-step process for telling better stories, I want to share something with you about the phrase "see a different universe." This phrase is meant to be taken literally. But seeing a different universe doesn't mean that pigs will fly, grass will be purple, and the Chicago Cubs will win the World Series (sorry Cubs fans, I couldn't resist). You will see physical, tangible changes to your material reality, such as a fit body, financial abundance, a loving soul mate, a satisfying career, a beautiful home—or any other unique desire you are willing to tell new stories about and align your beliefs with. When you change your beliefs by telling different stories, some things you see and experience will appear to be physically the same to you, but they will all hold new meaning for you. And, believe me, this will now provide you with just as much of the experience of seeing a new universe as will experiencing your fit body or fat bank account.

For example, when someone cuts you off in traffic, you won't say, "I hate that jerk. She has taken advantage of me and has made me angry." You'll say, "That person must feel like she has to get where she's going in a huge hurry. I feel sorry for her, since such actions almost always mean she's living a very stressful life."

When you look in the mirror, you won't say, "I'm ugly (or old, or fat, etc.)." You'll say, "I am a unique and beautiful person."

When you get some money, you won't say, "This isn't enough. It's not as much as I wanted, and I'm underpaid." You'll say, "Thank you for this contribution to my financial health. I'm grateful that my services are so valued that someone pays me for them."

When you get your electric bill, you won't say, "Oh great. Another damn bill, just when I was starting to get ahead." You'll say, "I'm so pleased to be able to exchange money for having my home provided with this amazing resource that I wouldn't want to live without."

When you wake up you won't say, "Oh no, another morning. I wish I could just stay in bed." You'll say, "Wow, a new day! I wonder what amazing adventures await me today."

When you're out in public, you won't say, "Look at all these strangers. I never meet anyone nice." You'll say, "Look at all wonderful people and opportunities. I wonder who I might meet and with whom I might exchange energy?"

When someone is rude or thoughtless to you, you won't say, "What a jerk. I wonder if they're acting that way because something is wrong with me." You'll say, "Some people, unfortunately, are scared and closed off. I feel empathy for this person, who's currently closed off to the positive energy of the universe, and I wish her well."

When you look at your partner, you won't say, "He annoys me so much sometimes. I wish he'd act the way I'd like him to." You'll say, "I am grateful to have a partner in whom I can invest my life. I'm going to treat him just as I'd like him to treat me today."

When you look at your child, you won't say, "Why doesn't she act like I want her to?" You'll say, "My daughter is doing the best she can and she's learning about life in her own way, just like I did. I'll continue to do my best to understand her and let her know I'm in her corner with all my support and love."

When you look at your car, you won't say, "I'm so tired of this old vehicle. Why can't I have a fancy car like the ones I see while driving to work?" You'll say, "I'm so grateful for my car. Perhaps someday I'll choose to get a new one, but, until that day, I'm grateful for this one."

Although I've used the word "say" in those examples, these won't just be things you'll simply be saying to yourself—they will not be platitudes. These will be your neural pathways of habitual thought and they will reflect what you believe because they will be who you have become. In other words, you will, literally, see these things (and many others) in your material reality and you won't have to force yourself to come up with these stories. You won't experience nearly as much disappointment and lack because you will see real opportunities where once you saw absence and obstacles. You will also, of course, see and experience the realization of many of your long-held dreams and goals, because not only will you have the inspiration and the opportunities to achieve them, you will also have become these things. You will be the living embodiment of many of your aspirations.

A good metaphor that illustrates the process of changing your beliefs to see a new universe is getting a college degree to enter a profession. If you enter college with the goal of becoming, let's say, an accountant, you will embark on a four-year program of coursework, study, and field experiences that all combine to confer that degree and title. As you successfully complete each component of your program, there is no single piece of it that is more important than the others. Each aspect of your four-year journey contributes to your degree in a small but essential manner. When you are finished and are awarded your degree and title, though, it is not the graduation ceremony, nor the degree itself, that really makes you an accountant. The degree does allow you to call yourself an accountant, but what really makes you an accountant is the fact that you know you are an accountant. You have become an accountant. And what makes you know you are an accountant is actually each one of those steps you have successfully completed during your unique four-year journey. You built yourself into knowing you are an accountant one class, one night of studying, and one internship at a time.

Becoming a successful person who sees a new universe happens in the same way. Your new beliefs are built through the process of telling new, better stories, using better, uplifting words. In the "end," when you have reached a satisfying level of achievement, it will not be the title, "slender, healthy person," "happily married person," or "financially successful person" that makes you that thing. The tangible results present in your material reality tell others that is what you are and allow you to call yourself that, but what makes you those things is the fact that you know you are those things. You have become those things. And what makes you know you are those things, just as with a college degree, is actually each of the new, better stories you have told yourself each day (and the new experiences those new stories have allowed you to have) during your unique process of reforming your neural pathways of habitual thought.

By the way, I placed quotes around the word "end" in the last paragraph because I have great news for you regarding the successful attainment of your dreams and goals using the architecture fish tank. There actually is no end to this process. You will find that, once you finally achieve your ideal body, move into that nice home, or develop that wonderful relationship (or any other of the myriad goals and dreams you have), entirely new desires will arise. You'll be inspired to dream of new, even bigger goals. And the best news about this is that you can be assured that this process of aligning your beliefs with your new goals continues to work your entire life—no matter how big and grand your dreams bloom. With the architecture paradigm there are no limits to how wonderful your fish tank can become. If you're so inspired, you will eventually inhabit SeaWorld.

Chapter Eleven: Six Tools to Keep Your Fish Tank Sparkling

"A physicist is an atom's way of knowing about atoms."

George Wald
Scientist
Nobel Prize Winner

This chapter will teach you six amazing tools you can use to put yourself in the best position possible to use your new architecture paradigm each day, telling better stories and growing your beliefs in the most wonderful ways.

You've undoubtedly already started seeing a more desirable universe and begun feeling differently about yourself and your life experiences by practicing the three steps you've learned about telling different stories. You're following through on your commitment to depersonalize your feelings and beliefs, telling better, uplifting stories using better, uplifting words. Congratulations! As you now know, the results of these changes are real. And, while you may not yet have achieved your dreams and goals as completely as you desire, you know that improvements begin to manifest immediately.

In addition to those three steps, I want to teach you some tools you can use that will make it even easier for you to change your beliefs and see a different universe for the rest of your life. These tools amplify the results you'll see from the architecture paradigm, making the changes more dramatic, impactful, and powerful. These tools will help you feel like you've replaced a rusty old handsaw with a heavy-duty chainsaw.

These tools, like the three steps for changing your beliefs, will become second nature and habitual with practice. At first, like the three steps, they may feel like a radical departure from the way you've always conducted yourself. But, even if they feel strange, trust that they will be of great help to you and apply yourself to them as thoroughly as you're able. They have been gleaned from years of studying with experts in self-growth like my father, Dr. Clifford Kuhn, Dr. Deepak Chopra, Dr. Wayne Dyer, and many others.

Time I suggest you take each one of these six tools and focus on that tool for a week. Every month and a half you'll have cycled through all of them and, after a year, you'll have spent eight weeks focused on each tool. If you commit yourself to that schedule while you practice the three steps for changing your beliefs, you won't even recognize your life after the year is over. And, in fact, you'll see amazing changes in your life and your material reality long before the year is up.

As with the three steps for changing your beliefs, take it easy on yourself with these six tools. Your goal is to practice them every day, as often as possible. But definitely do not beat up on yourself if you forget to practice them or if you feel like you're not getting as much from them as you should. And definitely remember to use kind, gentle words when you catch yourself forgetting to employ them. There is no expectation of mastery for these six tools. There is no time you'll be able to say, "I'm finished; I now practice them perfectly." Your goal is simply to get better and better at using them with each passing day, and also to experience the way your life improves as you practice.

Tool Number One - Always Tell the Best Story Possible

"If you have faith as small as a mustard seed, you can say to this mountain, 'Move from here to there' and it will move. Nothing will be impossible to you."

Matthew 17:20
The Bible

You already know that quantum science has taught us, beyond a shadow of a doubt, that there is no such thing as a detached observer. We all grew up with the image of a scientist watching an experiment and recording the data. But quantum physics tells us that this is impossible, because the observer acts as a direct participant in all that's being observed, which creates outcomes affected by the observer's expectations.

There are quantum experiments, with accuracy within 1/100 of a decimal point, showing us that the observer's expectations create the physical form that matter takes. Your expectations literally create the physical world around you. I realize this may be a huge shift for you and, perhaps, even hard for you to believe, but I assure you that quantum physics proves this definitively. So, even if you struggle to believe this data, allow me to help you begin using it to not only change your beliefs and see a different universe, but also to exponentially improve your fish tank in the process.

Telling yourself the best story possible is a phenomenal way to apply the discoveries of quantum physics, and it is a great tool for changing your beliefs. You already know that you tell stories about every person, place, thing, and circumstance in your life. You assign meaning to them. You designate each of them as being good or bad. There is nothing wrong with you telling these stories—it seems that's what you were born to do.

And, although you can choose what story you tell most of the time (especially with practice), you are not supposed to be able to magically make any person, place, thing, and circumstance good just because you have the freedom of choice. Certainly, masters of thought can transcend placing value and judgment upon life's events, but you and I are probably not going to be able to devote the energy, study, and practice necessary to join them.

This is why I am telling you to tell the "best story possible" at all times and not telling you to "always tell a good story."

When you discover that your beloved pet dog has been killed by an automobile, for example, you are not expected to be able to tell a story that makes that event good. For you, and almost every human, those types of life events are sad, frustrating, maddening, anguishing, and gut wrenching. If we're fully invested in our lives, such tragedy is supposed to feel that way.

However, if you're like most people, you can also think of many times when you interpreted fairly innocuous events as "bad." Not getting a phone call returned, someone breaking up with you, not getting a job, losing your electricity, or having a friend move away are all examples of things that you might've judged bad and told a bad-feeling story about when they occurred. Yet, with the passing of time, retrospect shows you that some of these things were actually good (or, at least, not nearly as bad as you judged them when they happened).

So remember this important tool each day and practice it as often as possible. Tell the best possible believable story for each person, place, thing, and circumstance you encounter. This means that you will not rush to label anything bad and, wherever possible, you will find a way to tell a good story about it. For example, when you don't get the job you wanted, instead of saying, "This is horrible; I never get what I want." you can tell this story: "This must not have been the job I'm supposed to get. Perhaps my best job is still out there and is still waiting for me."

A good way to visualize this tool is to imagine yourself as a director and the movie you're directing is your life. By telling the best stories possible, at all times, you are instructing the actors and support staff, setting the scenes, and directing the actions in the best possible ways— by giving meaning and value to all your life experiences that uplift you, motivate you, and serve the attainment of your dreams and goals. After all, since you are commanding the quantum field to manifest your material reality through your expectations, isn't this director analogy an apt one? And, since you're going to be directing your life each day, why would you choose to make a bad movie?

If you step on the scale and find, to your surprise, that you have gained two pounds, you don't have to tell a bad-feeling story and say, "I'm a failure." Instead you can choose a better feeling story like, "Although I am disappointed that I've gained two pounds instead of losing weight like I hoped, I can use my disappointment to motivate me tomorrow. In that way, these two pounds might end up being a blessing." But even if your story is not quite as good feeling as my examples, all you need to do, at any time, is simply tell the best possible story you can muster.

When a truly unwanted tragedy strikes, like your dog dying, of course the best possible story you can tell, at that moment, might be "This sucks!" That's okay; I never want you to pretend like you're not unhappy. If that's your best possible story (and I'm sure it would be for me, too) then you've done all you can and you've still used this tool to your fullest. Over the course of time, the story you can tell about such an emotional event will grow better and better.

And there is another reason that this tool is called "Always Tell the Best Story Possible" instead of "Always Tell a Good Story." It's because you should tell a story you'll believe. Believing your story is of paramount importance. For example, if you get fired from your job and, moments later, you try to tell yourself, "This doesn't suck. This is awesome! I'm so glad this happened." I doubt you could really believe that under almost any circumstances. But perhaps you might be able to believe a story like "This sucks. But I can choose to believe that, in the long run, I'll be okay and might even look back on this as a blessing." That feels better and remains believable, doesn't it? Or maybe the best story you can tell yourself is "This sucks. It won't feel bad forever, but it sure does suck right now." That's still believable and it certainly feels better than "I'm a failure. My life is ruined. Things never work out for me."

Here is a wonderful story that illustrates how one man told the best possible stories, even about tragic events, and how it changed his life for the better:

An African king had a close friend who had the habit of remarking, "This is good" about every occurrence in life, no matter what it was. One day, the king and his friend were out hunting. The king's friend loaded a gun and handed it to the king. But, alas, he loaded it wrong. And when the king fired it, his thumb was blown off.

"This is good!" exclaimed his friend.

The horrified and bleeding king was furious. "How can you say this is good? This is obviously horrible!" he shouted.

The king put his friend in jail.

About a year later, the king went hunting by himself. Cannibals captured him and took him to their village. They tied his hands, stacked some wood, set up a stake, and bound him to it. As they started to set fire to the wood, they noticed that the king was

missing a thumb. Being superstitious, they never ate anyone who was less than whole. They untied the king and sent him on his way.

Full of remorse, the king rushed to the prison to release his friend.

"You were right, it was good," the king said.

The king told his friend how the missing thumb saved his life, adding, "I feel so sad that I locked you in jail. That was such a bad thing to do."

"No! This is good!" responded his delighted friend.

"Oh, how could that be good, my friend? I did a terrible thing to you."

"It is good," said his friend, "because if I hadn't been in jail I would have been hunting with you and they would have eaten me!"

As quantum physics shows us, by looking for ways to feel as good as possible about people, places, things, and circumstances in your life, you are creating even more good in your life by telling yourself the best story possible.

As you practice telling the best story you can, you will not only continue building new beliefs and fully engaging the architecture paradigm, but you will also begin to see more good in everything you do. This is how the universe operates: It delivers what you expect to see rather than what you hope to see.

Tool Number Two - Focus on the Feelings You Want, Not the Actual Things You Want

"Very interesting theory - it makes no sense at all"

Groucho Marx
Comedian

One of the surest and fastest ways to bring anything into your experience is to concentrate on the feelings you'll have when you achieve your goal. Focusing on the goal, itself, usually brings up feelings of "Why isn't it here yet?" So make it your business to focus on the feeling you expect that goal to give you. This concept applies to anything in life you want.

Once again, this tool is a liberal application of something quantum physics has taught us: In the physical world, like attracts like. You've heard this principal discussed as the "law of attraction." I can assure you the law of attraction is actually real, and its underpinnings are found in the realm of science.

For our physical, human experience, we should pay attention to our feelings, for it is our feelings that tell us what we're attracting and bringing into our experience. Have you ever struck a tuning fork and heard how it vibrates? You probably know that a vibrating tuning fork will cause any other tuning fork, tuned to the same pitch, to begin vibrating in unison with it.

Think of your feelings as a tuning fork and think of the people, places, things, and experiences of your life as millions of tuning forks filling up the entire universe. When you ring your tuning fork, when you feel your feelings, all the tuning forks (the people, places, things, and experiences) that are tuned the same will begin to ring also. This is a literal explanation of the law of attraction in action.

As with the first tool, this one presents you with what might be a huge shift and might also be challenging for you to believe. But if you're willing to try this tool, I believe you'll find enough amazing results that you'll soon be an unqualified convert.

To start using this tool right away, create a list of good feelings you expect to have when you achieve your desired goals. Whatever your list consists of, it will become even more powerful if you write it down on a piece of paper. And try to feel those feelings, right now, as you write them down. Do not wait until something happens to "make" you feel these feelings; feel them for no "outside" reason at all. Try to feel them as often as possible each day, no matter what is going on around you. Give yourself permission to feel them right now and bask in their glow. To remind yourself, jot each list item on a small notepad and stick copies on your mirror, your desk at work, your computer screen, and your car dashboard.

Why will this work for you? If you're like most people, it has felt like you've been focusing on what you want, yet you've actually been focused on its absence—the fact that it is not there yet. If your goal is weight loss, for example, and the weight loss hasn't happened yet, you're constantly focused on some version of "Where is my weight loss? It's not here. I wish I would lose the weight." That is an example of focusing on the lack, or absence, of your desire.

And because like attracts like in our universe, you get what you focus on: "It's not here yet." Focusing on the feelings you want, by feeling those feelings as often as possible, will bring dramatic results.

By feeling the fantastic feelings you previously put off feeling, you are ringing your tuning fork at a new and different frequency, one that sounds like "I am successful, I am sexy, I am free, I am healthy, etc." And now, automatically, other tuning forks tuned to the same frequency will begin to vibrate in unison with you. Like-tuned people, places, things, and experiences will begin to manifest and come to you.

They will all be attracted to your feeling vibrations. It is the law of our universe.

Remember the old saying "I'll believe it when I see it?" You're going to find out that the correct way to state it is "I'll see it when I believe it." Because, by feeling the feelings of your success before the success is in your material reality, the universe will automatically begin bringing to you those people, places, things, and experiences that will make that success manifest in your material reality. It will feel like magic if you really make an effort to feel those feelings you listed as often as possible each day.

Take it easy on yourself as you practice this, though. You've spent your entire life looking at "what is" and focusing on the absence of the things you desire, saying, "Where is it?" Don't beat up on yourself when you lapse back into your old habits. Just take that as a reminder that you're not perfect yet (and aren't supposed to be) and start feeling your desired feelings again.

Tool Number Three - Meditate for Fifteen Minutes Each Day

"Man is the product of his thoughts. What he thinks, he becomes."

Mahatma Gandhi
Father of Indian Independence

Who are you? I can tell you, with almost complete certainty, who you are not. You are not your brain (even though your brain wants so badly to be who you are). And, in fact, your brain's struggle to be who you are has caused a lot of problems for you. You're about to get on the path to remedying those problems right now.

What I'm calling your brain, some refer to as your ego. Whichever term you use, if you're like most people you have spent your life listening to your brain's constant and incessant dialogue and you have come to believe that dialogue is "you." Your brain is pretty persuasive, and just about every human being falls for its act, so don't feel bad about getting duped.

However, for your brain to assume the identity of "who you are," your brain has to rely heavily upon fear and anger. You see, your brain has to get you to stay focused upon the future (obsessed about what might happen) and the past (obsessively rehashing everything that has happened and ruminating upon why it was good or bad). That is because your brain knows that who you really are can only be found in the present moment. So, in turn, your brain can only keep its identity as who you are by getting you out of the present moment.

Today, science understands that your brain is an elegant tool, more powerful and advanced than anything we can imagine. Yet it is only a tool, just like your heart, lungs, muscles, or nervous system. You make decisions every day. You decide to walk the stairs instead of taking the escalator, you decide to eat an apple instead of a cupcake, you decide to scratch your ear, you decide to turn left, etc. Your brain facilitates those decisions through your motor and sensory cortexes, but it does not make any decisions.

That's right, modern science has yet to find any part of your brain where decisions are made, only where they are carried out. Yet there is no doubt that there exists a "you" who is making decisions for your brain (and the rest of your body) to execute. This means that the real "you," the "you" that decides, is a non-physical energy. Call this energy what you will - God, your spirit, the universe, Brahma, source energy, Allah, Yahweh, the quantum field, etc. - the real "you" is non-physical, and that is becoming more difficult to deny.

Tool #3, meditation, allows you to meet the real "you," the non-physical you, and learn from your own wisdom. This tool helps you change your beliefs more rapidly and achieve your goals more quickly because being in contact with the real you, your non-physical energy, helps you feel calmer, more secure, more confident, more serene, more at peace, and happier. And feeling that way is like rocket fuel for your three steps for changing your beliefs, using the architecture paradigm and seeing a new, more desirable universe.

The good news is that all the benefits of meditation are simple to achieve - they only take willingness and practice. And practicing meditation requires, at most, 15 minutes a day.

Most of what I know about meditation is an amalgamation of what I've learned from Dyer and Chopra. There are many methods of meditation and many philosophies about it. Feel free to do whatever makes you most comfortable, even if your practice differs from mine. Ultimately, the most important thing about meditation is to still your mind, and however you find yourself best able to do that is wonderful.

Stilling your mind means choosing not to listen to the incessant chatter that your brain throws at you all day long. It has been said that your nonphysical energy can be found in the empty space between your thoughts. Meditation can be seen simply as an effective effort to widen the space between your thoughts. When you find the space between your thoughts, you'll find your true self—your nonphysical "you"—and it is in perfect alignment with all your dreams.

And here's a big reveal: The real, nonphysical "you" is already successfully experiencing your dreams and goals, choosing those experiences from the limitless, unformed potential of the quantum field, and is actually excited about the physical "you" experiencing that success too.

The way I meditate is very simple. I find a quiet spot and sit cross-legged, with my hands resting, upturned, on my knees and my thumbs and middle fingers touching. I close my eyes and imagine I'm sitting alone in a movie theater (there's that movie metaphor again). On the movie screen are the two words "I" and "Love." Then, in my mind's eye, I focus upon the empty space between the "I" and the "Love," all the while imagining good feelings shooting up my spine and escaping into the universe. When other thoughts arise, I don't freak out or get upset. I simply imagine a mild breeze blowing through my mind and gently whisking away my thoughts without any trouble.

Another method you might enjoy is to sit in the same comfortable style I just described and then imagine you're taking the top of your skull off, reaching into your cranium, and gently removing your brain. In your imagination, gently set your brain down beside you (I literally make the movements with my hands when I'm doing this) and lovingly tell your brain, "I'm not going to need you for the next fifteen minutes or so, my friend." Then sit quietly as a person with no brain and, therefore, no thoughts.

I do this for 15 minutes each day, preferably in the morning before I start into my daily routines and responsibilities. When you meditate, do so with no agendas or planned outcomes. Your goal is simply to spend as much of the 15 minutes as possible without thought, which is how you commune with your nonphysical "you."

The longer you practice meditation, you may notice something wonderful - you may find that you no longer need to set aside special, quiet time to access your non-judgmental, thought-less mind. You may find yourself more and more able to be quiet and without thought during all the portions of your day.

You'll find that, when you meditate, you're listening to the wisdom of the real "you," and that wisdom will often come in the form of feelings rather than words. Another wonderful benefit from your meditation practice is that the better you get at listening and communing with the real "you," the better you'll be able to listen to your gut and your instincts when it comes to your feelings and beliefs. You'll fool yourself into doing things that make you feel badly much less often because you're more in tune with your beliefs, your true nature, and how you really feel. If you're like me, you're going to find yourself falling in love with your nonphysical energy—which really means you'll be falling in love with yourself.

Tool Number Four - Still Your Mind as Often as Possible

"Mystics understand the roots of the Tao but not its branches; scientists understand its branches but not its roots. Science does not need mysticism and mysticism does not need science; but man needs both."

Fritjof Capra
Physicist

As you practice meditation each day and commune with your nonphysical energy, you will find yourself wanting to spend more and more time in between your thoughts because of all the freedom you find there. The energy of you, found in the empty space between your thoughts, is infinite, unbounded, and loving. It not only feels good spending time there, but being in touch with it also acts as a catalyst for making your dreams become real.

In your case, of course, you wish to change your beliefs to align with your desires so you can see a different universe and experience a physical reality more congruent with your dreams and goals. Realizing your dreams and goals is a desire you've had for many years, and has constantly eluded you because you spent most of your energy focused upon your actions rather than making sure you feel good about your actions before you do them. But trust me. The energy of the universe has heard your desire to achieve your goals. In fact, the universe has all your desired success just waiting for you to allow it to happen by aligning your beliefs with your dreams and goals.

The good news is that aligning your beliefs with your desires is exactly what you're doing right now by following the three steps to change them. And the even better news is that, even before it has become second nature for you to tell good stories about all your life experiences, there is a way to experience all the benefits of a completely positive, uplifting state of being.

In the absence of your telling nothing but good stories about everything you do, you can do something just as powerful: Tell no stories at all. Stilling your mind is just that: telling no stories. And when you still your mind, you have effectively turned off your brain and are making no judgments at all, which allows the universe to deliver to you all it has waiting for you in storage.

Stilling your mind is a form of waking, interactive meditation. The way you still your mind can be very simple. Just keep your attentions on your environment while you imagine a cool breeze blowing the thoughts right out of your head. You don't have to withdraw from your normal, daily activity to do this.

An additional way to still your mind works very well when driving. After all, you probably drive quite a bit each day, so this is a great opportunity for you to practice this tool. As I described in the previous tool, "Meditate for 15 Minutes Each Day," imagine you're taking the top of your skull off, reaching into your cranium, and gently removing your brain. Lovingly tell your brain, "I'm not going to need you right now, my friend" and imagine it sitting beside you in the passenger seat. Then drive without thought or judgment (while still paying attention to traffic, road signs, and directions).

You can still your mind anytime during your day for as long or as brief a time as you can get away with. And every time you still your mind, you will be in direct communion with your nonphysical energy - the real "you" who is waiting to present you with all the success you desire as soon as you allow your beliefs to align with those desires.

I like to think of it this way. Your blocked, unrealized desires are waiting for you in a giant lake of unrealized potential (the quantum field). The dam creating this lake is your resistance, your brain constantly telling bad stories that focus on "Where is it? It isn't here!" That dam is the only thing standing between you and the desires you have yet to see come to fruition. Each time you still your mind, you open a spigot that allows your blocked desires to begin flowing into your life experience. By stilling your mind, you neutralize all the negativity and resistance that is blocking your desires. How much flows and how long it flows out of that giant lake of blocked desires depends on how long and how often you still your mind each day.

In addition, you'll love the clarity and serenity you gain from stilling your mind. Shutting off your brain's constant clatter, if only for a few moments, can be like taking a long nap. It is incredibly refreshing and invigorating. And the more time you spend bonding with your true, nonphysical self, the more confidence you'll feel in the new you taking shape.

Tool Number Five - Feel Gratitude as Often as Possible

"Always remember that when you have committed yourself to an action, then the whole cosmos will conspire to help you. The keyword is commitment."

Mark Hedsel
Author

Of all the feelings in the world, there may be nothing more powerful than gratitude. If it were possible to feel gratitude at all times, I have no doubt that you would be a superhuman who made your desires manifest almost instantly. If you have any doubts about this, practice feeling gratitude as often as possible for a while and you'll soon see for yourself.

With this tool, you are now introduced to the most powerful tool imaginable for crafting good-feeling stories that serve you rather than hinder and block you.

Gratitude makes your stories feel amazingly good. And the good news is that you can feel grateful for anything and for any reason. To start, begin by looking at things you've become accustomed to taking for granted. Certainly your ability to breath, walk, talk, imagine, love, eat, and dream are just a few things that you can choose to feel grateful for right now. After all, you aren't guaranteed that you'll continue to have any of those gifts you are currently enjoying.

It's impossible to feel gratitude without feeling good.

When you have had a taste of gratitude for the "little things" you once habitually took for granted, move on to gratitude for the "small" victories. If you desire weight loss, eating one doughnut instead of three before you realize you don't feel good about that is something to be grateful for. Sure, you can beat yourself up for eating the one doughnut, but doesn't finding gratitude in your growth feel better? And isn't beating yourself up a cardinal "no-no" for following the three steps to change your beliefs because it personalizes your feelings and beliefs, investing them with too much emotional power?

Going outside today and walking around your block when you haven't done so in years is cause for gratitude, too. Who cares if you didn't do it at a record pace? Pat your back and say, "Way to go, me!" Feel grateful for the movement you did rather than feeling bad for having walked "only a block."

As you begin feeling grateful for the "little things" you once called "not enough," you'll really be on the track to greatness. For example, I may not run as much as a really dedicated athlete, but I am grateful for my ability and opportunities to go on a two- or three-mile jog. Nobody (except me) can tell me that's not enough movement. And, because I'm choosing to be grateful for all my movement today, I know I'm doing enough.

Once you've gotten practice feeling grateful for the things you once took for granted and for the "little" things that once felt like they weren't enough, you'll be ready for the major leagues of gratitude. Here, you'll start telling yourself the best stories you can ever imagine.

Gratitude will become almost your secret super-power. You can now begin to completely make your own rules about being grateful.

For example, spiritualists and physicists alike both teach us that two opposite experiences, such as "giving" and "receiving," are really the same exact experience—they are just being viewed from two different perspectives.

This example shows you that you are free to make your own rules. You can actually choose to be grateful for anything you experience (yes, even the "unwanted" things) if you decide to see it as merely the opposite perspective of something you desire more. Another example is finding gratitude in experiences you would normally label bad because you choose to see them as necessary contrasting experiences that are showing you what you don't want, motivating you to make the changes necessary to get what you do want.

By making your own rules for gratitude, you can begin to actually feel grateful for your unwanted experiences. Sound crazy? Who made the rules that you have to feel bad about your unwanted experiences and that you can't feel grateful for them? Later, I'll reveal why I'm so grateful for some undesirable experiences I've had. I'll suggest that, if you so choose, you can find reasons to feel grateful for yours too— perhaps because it's given you motivation to make these changes and reasons to learn and grow in unexpected ways.

I extend my right to feel grateful for anything I choose to all areas of my life. If you're like me, you'll learn that no one will punish you, scold you, or put you in time-out for feeling grateful about anything. In fact, if you're like me, you'll be infused with energy and a connection to the real, nonphysical you when you remember to be grateful. You, too, may find that gratitude is addictive because of the way feeling good about yourself brings wonderful results into your life.

I promise you that when you get to the point where you are looking for ways to feel grateful for most things you experience (and you will, with practice) you will be well on your way to never having to experience a lack of personal success and fulfillment again.

Tool Number Six - Create and Celebrate Success

"We don't know what electricity is, or what gravitation is, although we use and live by it every day. Miracles are everywhere. Why look for them? Just let them in."

Jo Michel
Artist

The sixth tool, Create and Celebrate Success, picks up where practicing gratitude left off. A commitment to practicing gratitude leads to creating successes. And practicing gratitude also leads to celebrating your successes. Creating and celebrating your success, in turn, presents more and more opportunities for gratitude. And that's a wonderful circle to be caught up in.

My Father, Clifford Kuhn, M.D., The Laugh Doctor, teaches a beautiful Smile Strategy he calls "Celebrate Everything." Celebrating everything gives you the greatest opportunity to feel grateful and appreciative. With this tool, I am asking you to take celebrating yourself and your accomplishments to uncharted territory. Similar to what I asked you to do with gratitude, I want you to create things to celebrate—simply because you can! Because celebrating will fill you with positive energy and open yourself up to receive even more from your reservoir of blocked desires.

I want you to celebrate things you would normally have barely acknowledged, such as someone smiling at you, paying a bill, finding a dime on the sidewalk, or someone complimenting you on how you look. Pump up the volume for such events and pat yourself on the back till you're sore. In fact, I recommend that you literally pat yourself on the back. As you start doing this more and more, you'll start to feel like your own biggest fan and you'll find that's an incredible motivation to keep moving forward.

Also begin to look for celebrations you would have normally overlooked but that recognize a change in the stories you're telling and a change in your behavior. Celebrate things like not using ugly words in your stories, telling a better story about something undesirable, saying something nice about yourself when you see your reflection, and referring to yourself kindly. Celebrate the times you think, "I have unwanted weight" instead of "I am fat." Celebrate feeling a little excitement about the new actions you're inspired to take toward the achievement of your dreams and goals. Celebrate anytime you tell a better feeling story.

Think about how you teach a child to ride a bike. You wouldn't put her on a bike and say, "Go to it" while you watched from the porch, would you? And you certainly wouldn't chastise her when she messed up and fell over. You'd encourage and celebrate every little bit of progress she made, starting with her being able to sit on the bike seat, to her pedaling for a few feet (even with your steady hand on her back). Celebrating a child's successes helps her gain confidence and builds a skill that you know she'll eventually master. But there's only one way to get there: by practicing. By making mistakes and experiencing one little success after another until, finally, she reaches her goal.

You know that the best way to teach a child is not to chastise her for making a mistake. So why not give yourself that same nurturing care and encouragement? Anticipate your desire to celebrate success on your journey to realize your desired outcomes. Plan achievable goals and also plan to celebrate those achievements. As you meet a new friend for the first time, celebrate by going out for coffee later that day. As you eat a salad for lunch instead of a burger and fries, celebrate by seeing a funny movie that evening.

And lose the requirement that others join in with you. Who cares if no one else wants to celebrate with you or even if people pooh-pooh your celebrating as frivolous? Feel sorry for them and continue. And, if you need to, simply keep your celebrations private.

Take celebrating seriously and you'll see seriously good results from it. More gratitude. More energy. And better stories too, which means more powerful alignment between your beliefs and your desires. In fact, a great way to use this tool is to cultivate a group of friends to whom you can openly and wantonly "brag" about yourself without having to apologize or throw in statements of unnecessary humility. Get some friends who'll let you toot your own horn as loudly and proudly as you can while understanding that you're doing it because it's good to celebrate yourself.

Chapter Twelve: Welcome to Your New Aquarium

"Nothing in life is to be feared. It is only to be understood."

Marie Curie
Scientist
Nobel Prize Winner

It took me 15 years to learn to fully use the architecture fish tank as you're doing now. You'll find success much sooner than that, because you won't have to make all the mistakes I did. And not only will you achieve any dream or goal you decide to and be able to maintain it, in doing so you will enter the prime of your life. As a good friend of mine who lost over 100 pounds using the architecture paradigm likes to say, "If, when I started this lifestyle, I'd written down everything I thought I'd get out of it, I'd have severely shortchanged myself."

I'm now going to share two examples of how the architecture fish tank, and the three-step process to fully use it, has worked in my life. The first one, about weight loss, is an illustration of a rather seamless application of this paradigm, while the second, concerning financial abundance, is one illustrating just how important it is to apply your life to the three-step process you've learned.

Here's an example of how changing my paradigms and my stories about eating worked for me. I used to talk and obsess about what foods were bad for me. I counted calories, carbohydrates, and fat grams. Then I would deprive myself of all the good-tasting food that I craved because it was bad for me to eat. Consequently, I would force myself to eat the bad-tasting food I didn't want because I thought it was good for me to eat it. Bear in mind that I was the sole source of, and bore full responsibility for, my stories of what foods were good and what foods were bad. Certainly, I based my stories on diet and nutrition literature, but it was I who made the choice to adopt and believe those stories.

Now you might say, "But that literature was written by licensed, credentialed experts who knew their stuff about food and health. Doesn't that mean you should have listened to them and believed them?" And I will counter by reminding you that our universe does not work on action but on energy. So the real question is not whether I should have believed the stories of the experts but whether I felt good about the stories I was telling myself based on that literature. And my answer to that question was a resounding no. The stories I told myself after listening to the food experts did not feel good.

So, under these circumstances, I was faced with two choices: Either I stopped eating any foods about which I couldn't tell any good-feeling stories or I learned to tell better feeling stories about foods I wished to continue eating. Since I believed the experts were correct about fresh vegetables and fruit being good for my body and fat and excess calories being bad for my body, I chose to begin telling myself better feeling stories about fresh vegetables and fruit.

By this point, I was eating fresh fruit in the morning instead of doughnuts or pancakes (some of my old favorites), but I just didn't naturally feel good about eating fresh fruit. It did not feel realistic to tell myself a story like "I love eating fresh fruits and I never want to go back to eating doughnuts and pancakes in the morning. I am so glad I have found this wonderful new way to eat in the morning." But I was able to tell myself a story like "Just for today, I am willing to eat fresh fruit this morning. I give myself permission to decide again tomorrow whether I want to continue, but I can do this for one day." I told myself that story each morning for weeks and I did begin to slowly feel better about eating fresh fruit.

But I didn't stop there. After a week or so, I began to add to my story: "And I can also believe that it's possible for me to start enjoying the consumption of fresh fruit just as much as I enjoy the consumption of doughnuts and pancakes. I don't enjoy fruit as much right now, but I'm willing to believe that I can eventually." At that point, that better-feeling story felt realistic, and I soon felt even better about eating all that fresh fruit.

As my good feelings about eating fresh fruit grew, it started to feel realistic to add still more good-feeling stories, such as "I am pretty confident that I can find fruits that I enjoy during each season and, perhaps, even come to anticipate the arrival of them as their season approaches." That story felt great, and by this time, after months of eating fresh fruit, it felt completely believable. And, for the first time in my life, I was actually excited about eating fresh fruit.

As my feelings improved and I was no longer spending anywhere near the energy telling myself bad-feeling stories about missing the old foods, I started to experience different results with my body. My beliefs and, thus, my expectations, were changing, and the universe was responding in small but noticeable ways. For example, I noticed I had more physical energy since starting to eat fresh fruit in the morning. In addition, I began to see that some of my unwanted weight was leaving. I also felt proud of myself for nourishing my body so lovingly.

Momentum was building.

Within six months, I was telling myself stories like "I love eating fresh fruits and I never want to go back to eating doughnuts and pancakes in the morning. I am so glad I have found this wonderful new way to eat in the mornings." And I knew these stories were true to the core of my soul. They had become my reality; I had successfully changed my beliefs. And I had done it one story at a time—not trying to jump up to the best feeling stories at first, but working my way up by telling myself the best feeling stories that felt believable to me every step of the way.

I did the same thing with fresh vegetables, organic foods, healthier options when eating out, and eating less fat, salt, and grease. I now honestly do not even like to eat anything but fresh fruit in the mornings. I love fresh vegetables (steamed and without any butter on them) and I do not like fast food anymore at all. These good feelings about such healthy fare reflect my new beliefs. They serve me and uplift me and they feel fantastic. I almost never feel deprived anymore, nor do I have to force myself to stick to any certain diet, because I have learned to feel great about what I eat. I am even able to eat ice cream and doughnuts today without experiencing unwanted weight gain. I have learned how to eat those foods in moderation and feel good about doing it.

And, over time, I've created new beliefs about exercising just the same way I did about eating—one story at a time. You know how I can tell? Because, unlike my previous experiences as a younger man, I now get excited when I think about exercising. Because exercising is fun and it is wonderful to have the opportunity to move my body and be healthier. Those are my beliefs now.

And I did it by telling myself the best possible stories about my eating and movement, starting with how I really felt and slowly improving those stories over time to the point where I now have some phenomenal beliefs about eating that really serve me and my body beautifully. My beliefs have allowed me to take off all my unwanted weight. Gone. And I have kept it off, with ease, for about 15 years now.

This next example, about changing my beliefs about money is more painful, yet it is very important as it shows you just how vital it is to apply your life to the three steps exactly as I've taught you. I used to be obsessed with becoming wealthy, yet financial abundance was always frustratingly absent from my material reality. Most of my adult life, any time I acquired more money, it always disappeared quickly, seemingly slipping through my fingers without ever allowing me to have used it in the ways I wanted to. I desired to be rich and live without debt and, to that end, I not only tried to live on a budget, but I also always pursued side businesses to enhance the income from my job. Yet, despite, my efforts, prior to reforming my neural pathways of habitual thought about money, I stayed in debt and was frustrated by the absence of more money in my material reality.

Seeing someone drive a BMW past me on the freeway often drove me mad with jealousy. I made a good salary and worked hard on my side businesses, yet I could never get ahead financially and was always three steps behind where I wanted to be. Finally, in 1999, I found a business idea I thought was foolproof and, after talking it over with my wife, decided to sink everything into it. I already knew that I created my material reality through my expectations, so I naïvely thought that all I had to do was take a big leap and simply think nothing but positive thoughts about the business. I thought, "This is it. This is the big break I've been seeking, and I need to show my faith in my personal power to manifest abundance by going 'all in' with no reservations. I know how to create my own reality. All I need to do is take this big action and I'll finally become wealthy." I did not yet understand how vital it was to truly change my beliefs on a deep and lasting level (as you now know to do), so my decision was unwittingly foolish (so much for foolproof, huh?) and almost cost me everything.

Looking back on my decision, I know that my mistake was in misunderstanding how the architecture paradigm really works. I want to stress that I've since corrected this mistake and the plan for using the architecture fish tank you've learned reflects the changes I made and the financial abundance I now experience. You won't make similar errors if you adhere to the three-step process you've learned, yet it will be very helpful for you to learn from my painful errors.

As I've written, when I made the fateful decision to invest everything I had into what turned out to be a too-good-to-be-true business endeavor, I knew all about these paradigms from quantum physics. But as I've also written, I did not yet understand just how important it is to change your beliefs on a deep level as you've now been taught. I took action toward fulfilling my dream of wealth by sinking all my resources into that business with the foolhardy belief that all I had to do was commit myself to thinking nothing but positive thoughts about it. So I made it my job to constantly and continually shower myself with positive affirmations and statements about my business's success. I spoke about my business only in positive ways, I meditated about my business with positive feelings and intent, and I read lots of uplifting books to inspire my thoughts and keep them 100% positive.

So when everything came crashing down on me and my family a few years later—and all my previous resources and assets were transformed into crushing debts and obligations, I was beyond devastated. I could not conceive how these paradigms had "failed" me after I had legitimately put so much effort into nothing but positivity. As I started to clean up the huge financial mess I had created, though, I learned some of the most valuable lessons of my life and I was also able to craft the architecture paradigm that has served me so amazingly ever since.

One of the primary lessons I learned, as I mentioned earlier, is that unless we change our beliefs, all the positive statements and affirmations in the world will only amount to a thin, almost useless, veneer covering our ocean of negativity. For it is from our true beliefs that our material reality is manifesting. Positive thoughts, without investing ourselves in a process to truly change our beliefs, will not actually command the universe to create a different reality for us. This is precisely why I've taught you in Step Three to listen deeper than simply your top-of-mind awareness about your beliefs concerning your dreams and goals. If your dreams and goals have been absent, that means that your true beliefs about them cannot be congruent with your desires. If you had asked me how I felt about money in 1999, as I made those awful investments, I would have sworn to you that I loved money and passionately wanted more of it. Yet, after my failed business, as I began to create and practice the plan you've learned in this book, I discovered my true beliefs about money. When I actually took the time to listen to my gut, my true beliefs about money were "I'm not worthy of more than I have," "It's greedy and bad to want more then I have," etc. Knowing what I do now about the architecture fish tank, it was literally impossible to experience abundant wealth in my material reality with those beliefs. No amount of surface-level statements and affirmations of positivity could overcome that incongruence between my beliefs about money and my desire for money.

Fueled by the need to clean up the financial mess I'd created, I began the actual process you've learned of reforming my neural pathways of habitual thought concerning money. My commitment to tell better stories about money, using uplifting words, started right where I was. To that end, my stories about money were initially along the lines of "Although I currently believe that financial abundance is bad and beyond my grasp, I also believe that, over time and with practice, I can change those beliefs by telling better stories about money. And, as I change my beliefs about money, I also believe that I can experience an eventual change in my material reality."

Here are some examples of the new stories I chose to tell about money to reform my beliefs:

"Bills are not actually bad if I choose to think of them as me exchanging my money for a wonderful and necessary service or resource that I'm grateful to receive."

"Finding a penny on the ground can be a cause for celebration if I choose to view that as a reminder of the infinite responsiveness, creativity, and abundance of the quantum field as it responds to my beliefs."

"While the amount of this check may be less than I hope to eventually receive for my efforts, I can choose to celebrate this money being shared with me and I believe that the more I celebrate what I currently have, instead of telling myself it's not enough, more money will come into my material reality over time."

Did these stories immediately produce a physical reality that reflected my ultimate desires about financial abundance? No, not at first. But I did notice an immediate improvement in small but tangible ways. As the better stories started improving my beliefs, the better I felt about money. And the better I felt about money, the more I became inspired to tell and believe still better stories. The continued, incremental growth of money into my material reality, as well as the better stories, became like a snowball rolling down a hill, growing in size as it traveled faster and faster.

By the time I'd been telling better stories about money for about eight months, I was not only experiencing more money in my material reality, but I was also inspired to tell even better stories that were completely believable such as, "Although the money I'm currently experiencing in my physical reality is not as great as my ultimate desires, I know that my beliefs are continuing to grow and I know that my ultimate destination is to experience the money I've dreamt of. The only variable is time as I practice telling still better stories about money, and I can choose to enjoy the ride rather than focus on what hasn't materialized yet. I do not have to believe that I must wait until my desires have fully manifested to be happy and grateful about my increasing financial abundance right now." You probably are correctly surmising that these improved stories brought about not only a continued growth of money in my material reality, but also stoked the fire of inspiration to continue this process of living the architecture paradigm.

Within a year and a half of this process, I had truly realized my financial desires—experiencing more money than I ever had. By then, the stories I told myself were akin to "I know that financial abundance is mine. I embody and expect financial abundance. Wealth is who I am. Money loves me, and I love it in return." These stories had become my beliefs and I had not only materialized enough money and resources to clear away over $800,000 in debt, but I was also watching my checking and saving accounts swell. Today, years later, I almost always experience a happy abundance of financial freedom. Having been faced with looming bankruptcy and foreclosures in 2003, I now live with my large, happy family in a wonderfully located, expansive, beautiful home, own another gorgeous home in a highly desirable neighborhood, live relatively debt-free, and enjoy a lifestyle with my family that affords us almost everything we desire (including the ability to fulfill our commitment to helping others).

Does this mean that I have more money than I know what to do with (including helping family, friends, and charity)? Does it mean that I never encounter a frustrating or unexpected bill or debt? Not at all. But, because of my new beliefs, I no longer experience any temporary lack of money as some link in a maddeningly unbreakable chain of absence. I am truly able to see such temporary circumstances as opportunities to both reexamine my beliefs about money and continue to grow my beliefs by telling better stories. I have more money in my life today than I have ever experienced, and I expect (and know) that my financial abundance will only continue to grow.

You see, just as I described earlier, as my dreams have been realized (in many areas of my life), so too have those dreams continued to grow. And I've learned, as you will, that with a commitment to the architecture paradigm and a resolve to continue following the three-step process of changing your beliefs, I am also continually seeing a more desirable universe with each passing month. And you will also find, as I do, that as your stories and your beliefs improve, you'll not only be blessed with increased motivation and inspiration to take new actions, but you'll also experience people and opportunities, often appearing out of the blue, that will further and enhance the achievement of your dreams and goals. What makes that last statement even more exciting is that I've found I am ultimately just as much a resource to these people and opportunities as they are to me. My life consists of a cocreative process where everyone can benefit, grow, and help one another. And this process of cocreation only further inspires and enhances the stories I tell, the beliefs I hold, and the abundance I experience in every area of my life.

I truly can't wait for you to have these experiences too when you realize your unique dreams and goals. Remember to be patient with yourself regarding how quickly your desires manifest into your material reality. How rapidly you experience your dreams will ultimately depend on how much willingness you have to help your beliefs align with them. You probably shouldn't expect your ultimate desires to manifest overnight, but you can rest assured that they will materialize as your beliefs become more congruent with your goals. And you can buoy yourself with the knowledge that your material reality, your universe, will start to change the moment you start telling better stories that reflect your changing expectations, as long as you adhere to the three-step process for changing your beliefs and using the architecture paradigm.

What is my life like today, fully applying it to the architecture fish tank and living the three-step process of reforming my neural pathways of habitual thought by telling better stories? Not only do I experience more love, joy, and fulfillment in my relationships, career, finances, health, and fitness than I ever dreamed, I've even learned to enjoy finding limiting beliefs that occasionally inhibit the material realization of my dreams and goals. Why do I enjoy finding limiting beliefs today? Am I crazy? Actually, the answer is simple: As I realize and attain my desires, I expect those desires to continue to grow and expand into even grander ones. Yes, I embrace finding limiting beliefs today because this simply means my dreams have continued to grow and it's now time to tell even better stories so my beliefs can become aligned with my even greater dreams and goals. As a friend of mine says when he encounters a goal he can't achieve, "It's merely time to tell a better story."

Isn't that a beautiful example of practicing the tool of gratitude? I can actually find genuine, believable gratitude in limiting beliefs (and, as of yet, unrealized desires) by looking at them merely as signals that I can achieve even more than I currently am. And there is no reason for me to feel any other way about such things since I am secure in the knowledge of how to change my beliefs. Nothing is out of reach for me today if I desire it. And you, too, can choose to follow my lead by incorporating this type of gratitude into your stories right now. Isn't it also possible for you to tell yourself such a story about being grateful for your nonaligned beliefs and unrealized desires, since they have ultimately led you to this book? And now, having learned how the universe works and your physical reality is created, you have the solutions in your hands to begin changing your beliefs to match those unrealized desires and to experience the realization of your previously absent dreams and goals. You have every tool you need and all you have to do is start practicing, have patience, and be kind to yourself along the way. When it comes to achieving some of your most precious desires, the only variable for you, now, is time. With dedication and diligence it will happen for you as surely as every other law of our universe.

If you want the type of life I've described myself as having, I encourage you to dream even bigger. You don't necessarily have to settle for what I am achieving! And I sincerely hope you choose to contact me and share your journey, revealing your better stories and the improvements in your material reality you experience. In this way, I can grow with you in a cocreative process; you can help me as much as I have helped you. You see, I have learned that abundance of any kind is not a zero-sum game; your success in any endeavor does not limit mine. Success is not a pie of predetermined size whereby increasing the size of your slice, you reduce mine. I love to help and share in other's successes, because they are great reminders to me of the unlimited creativity and responsiveness of the quantum field. Remember how I described feeling jealousy when I saw a beautiful BMW? Now, when I see an expensive luxury car, I say, "Thank you for sharing your abundance with me and allowing me to experience your success vicariously. Thank you for reminding me that the only limitations on my successes and achievements are the ones I impose on myself through limiting beliefs I choose to hold."

I have learned that the quantum field always gives you what you believe and expect. Whatever you believe, the quantum field always gives it to you exactly as you expect it. It can be frustrating to realize, however, that what you expect and what you desire can be two different things.

My successes and achievements have almost nothing to do with my actions when compared to the importance of my beliefs. As quantum physics teaches us, it's not about the action, it's about the energy. And, in fact, I encourage you to not try to figure out how your dreams and goals will materialize because, as I've written earlier, as your beliefs change, new people and opportunities will arrive to further you dreams just when they're supposed to. Part of seeing a different universe, as you now know, is seeing opportunities that probably always existed but were kept hidden by your previous limiting beliefs.

Write the following on a piece of paper and tape it to your desk, your dashboard, your bathroom mirror, and above your kitchen sink:

1. I hold beliefs.

2. My beliefs create my expectations.

3. The quantum field delivers exactly what I expect (which, as I know, is not always in alignment with what I desire).

4. My feelings tell me whether my beliefs are in alignment with my desires. If I feel good, I am in alignment; if I feel bad, I am not.

5. My feelings are like my thermometer, telling me how much my beliefs are in (or out) of alignment with my desires. Good feelings let me know that my beliefs and desires are aligned, while bad feelings let me know that my beliefs and desires are not aligned. And how intense the good or bad feeling is indicates how closely aligned (or how greatly separated) my beliefs and desires are.

6. The solution to being out of alignment with my beliefs is to change what I know. I do this by consistently deciding to always tell myself the best story I can possibly believe, using uplifting words to tell my stories.

Practice telling the best story possible about all the people, places, things, and circumstances you encounter. Over time, you will find that your beliefs will change about lots of things. Things that used to automatically signal you to feel like a loser, unlucky, or down in the dumps won't make you feel so bad. You'll be training yourself to see more and more clearly the gifts and blessings inherent in everything, because, as your stories change, your beliefs will change.

As your beliefs become more closely aligned with your desires, you will feel optimism, find gratitude, and will see the gifts in almost all your life's circumstances. And you will experience much more of what you want from life. That is because, as your beliefs change, the universe will change with them. As you feel better about yourself, you will manifest things more and more closely aligned with your desires. Relationships, peace, serenity, career opportunities, financial abundance, health, and self-acceptance can be found, as the joys of the universe automatically manifest in response to your new beliefs, which are now much more in line with your strongest desires.

This process, as described in this book, is your prescription for using the amazing science of quantum physics in your life, right now, to change yourself and your world. By following this process, you are plugged in to the way the universe really functions. Through the two new architecture paradigms, you will not—in fact, you cannot – fail, because quantum physics is so wonderfully and incredibly accurate and precise. You are becoming that person with the life you fantasized about.

And, if you're like me, you will discover that the quantum field has always been infinite, abundant, and ready to deliver all those wonderful things to you. Even when you felt your worst about yourself, those things were still available to you because they are your birthright. The stream of good will didn't increase through your practice of telling better stories (it couldn't get any larger!); only the size of the bucket you dip into the stream of good will increased.

You see, you are the bucket that gets dipped into the universe's stream of good will. And the size of your bucket is dictated by how much self-worth you feel; the greater your self-worth, the bigger the bucket you dip into the stream. Now that your self-worth is on the rise, you're going to be shouting with joy, "Fill 'er up, universe!"

And you're going to love what you find.

About the Author

Author Greg Kuhn is a professional educator and a futurist, specializing in framing new paradigms for 21st- century living. For the last 15 years, he has written primarily with his father, Dr. Clifford Kuhn, M.D., about health, wellness, and productivity.

Greg lives in Louisville, Kentucky, with a wonderful wife and four fantastic sons (one by marriage) whom he couldn't have published this book without. You can read more at:

Greg's blog - www.whyquantumphysicists.wordpress.com

Greg's Tweets- @KuhnGregory

Future books in Greg's "Why Quantum Physicists…" series will cover:

* Teaching

* Financial abundance

* Romantic relationships

* Parenting

* Blending Families

Greg gives talks and presentations for these topics tailored for both adult and youth audiences. If you'd like to inquire about his availability, simply contact him via email (laughdrjr@insightbb.com) or through the sites previously listed. Feel free, also, to contact Greg and suggest additional topics for his "Why Quantum Physicists…" series.